# EARLY SYRIAC THEOLOGY

## With Special Reference to the Maronite Tradition

### Msgr. Seely J. Beggiani

D1430874

UNITY
PRESS OF
AMERICA

LANHAM • NEW YORK • LONDON

Copyright © 1983 by

University Press of America,™ Inc.

4720 Boston Way
Lanham, MD 20706

3 Henrietta Street
London WC2E 8LU England

Library of Congress Cataloging in Publication Data

Beggiani, Seely J., 1935–
  Early Syriac theology.

    Bibliography: p.
    1. Theology, Doctrinal–History–Early church, ca.
30-600. 2. Fathers of the church, Syriac. 3. Catholic
Church–Maronite rite–Doctrinal and controversial
works. I. Title.
BT25.B37        1983       230'.14              83–3658
ISBN 0–8191–3152–0
ISBN 0–8191–3153–9 (pbk.)

In Memory

of my Parents

Joseph and Sada Beggiani

## ACKNOWLEDGEMENTS

The author wishes to express his thanks to Archbishop Francis M. Zayek for giving him the opportunity and the encouragement to pursue this project. He is also grateful to his fellow faculty members at Catholic University of America for their support. Special thanks go to Rev. Alfred McBride, O. Praem., who read the manuscript and offered helpful suggestions.

Acknowledgement is made to the following authors and publishers for permission to use material under copyright:

To Oxford University Press for permission to use Three Monophysite Christologies: Severus of Antioch, Philoxenus of Mabbug, and Jacob of Sarug by Roberta Chesnut, copyright 1976.

To Archbishop Francis M. Zayek, Bishop of St. Maron, and Rev. Joseph Amar for permission to use Lectionary, Syriac-Maronite Church, The Seasons, copyright 1976, and Anaphora Book of the Syriac Maronite Church of Antioch, copyright 1978.

To Sebastian Brock for permission to use his book, The Harp of the Spirit (Fellowship of St. Alban and St. Sergius, 1975), and his articles, "Ephrem's Letter to Publius", Le Museon, vol. 89 (1976) pp. 261-305; and "Baptismal themes in the writings of Jacob of Serugh," Orientalia Christiana Analecta, vol. 205 (1978) pp. 325-47.

To the editors of Sobornost (which incorporates Eastern Churches Review), St. Basil's House, 52 Ladbroke Grove, London W11 2PB, England, for permission to use "A Hymn of St. Ephrem to Christ on the Incarnation, the Holy Spirit, and the Sacraments,", by Robert Murray, S.J., Eastern Churches Review, vol. 3 (1970-1) pp. 142-50; and "Mary, the Second Eve in the Early Syriac Fathers," by Robert Murray, S.J., Eastern Chruches Review, vol. 3 (1970-1) pp. 372-84.

## TABLE OF CONTENTS

# FOREWARD

The pluralism advocated in the Catholic Church today is a reflection of a similar variety of world-views in its origins. The Eastern churches as well as the Western church are the ongoing representatives of the cultures and world-views of peoples of the first few centuries after Christ who first responded to the Gospels. The development of theology within each of these various traditions has its own history and was affected by external and internal factors and events.

The area of concentration of this work is the "early Syriac period". The choice of this period and region is due to my desire to trace the roots of the theology of the Maronite church. Historically the Maronite church can trace its origins to Syria, followed by its eventual establishment in Lebanon. Juridically, it situates itself in the see of Antioch. On the other hand, the development of the Maronite liturgical tradition is more complex. As we shall discuss later, Maronite liturgy may have had its origins in an original Chaldean rite that was subsequently affected by the Antiochene tradition. It later underwent inroads from Latin influences.

The starting point for a Maronite theology is to be located before the period of Latin influence, which began with the Crusades and became more intense in the sixteenth century. Much of what was written after the arrival of the Latins was merely an adaption or translation of Latin works into Syriac and Arabic. On the other hand, if theological works were written prior to the Latin period, they have not survived. Therefore, in attempting to formulate a Maronite theology, one cannot deal with specifically theological sources, but rather should examine the rich treasures to be found in the liturgy and the divine office. In fact, a special feature of Maronite worship is the 'prayer of incense' or 'hoosoyo' which usually expresses theologically either the events of salvation history or the meaning of the sacraments/mysteries being celebrated. Maronite liturgy began to develop its charactersitic form and content in the fourth century. In doing so, it incorporated the theological thought of Syriac writers of that time period, the time of Aphraat and Ephrem.

It is my presumption that a study of the theological insights of these writers and their immediate successors such as James of Serug, Philoxenus of Mabboug, and Narsai will provide an adequate context for understanding the theological origins of the Maronite tradition.

This work being a survey claims only to deal with selected issues in a general way. No study is made of the Syriac writings of the second and third centuries. It is hoped that the authors we are considering represent the fruition of early Syriac thought. On the other hand, the theological developments of the seventh century onwards can provide material for a subsequent work. The Latin insertions in later Maronite liturgical texts are now being removed in the present reforms of the liturgy.

The Syriac authors that we are studying did not express themselves by rational speculation or systematization, but rather by the use of a range of symbols and images, and by paradox. With roots in Judeo-Christianity, their theology was fundamentally biblical in thought and expression. At times, they even expressed hostility to Greek philosophy. Our attempts to systematize their thought can hope to be only partially successful. The use of such categories as God, creation, revelation, incarnation, etc. are not always adequate to the task and involve overlapping, but was done out of convenience. Often where the thought of our writers defied systematization, I have resorted to lengthy citations or paraphrases.

In the course of presenting this survey of early Syriac thought, examples are drawn almost exclusively from the Maronite liturgy and office. Similar examples could have been cited from the other Antiochene and Chaldean liturgies. As has been stated, the principal purpose of this work is to seek the origins of Maronite theology, and to help Maronites to come to a better understanding of their tradition. However, since the Maronites share their roots with other peoples of the Syriac world, and are a significant element in the pluralism of traditions that is the Catholic Church, it is hoped that this work will be of interest to a larger audience.

# INTRODUCTION

## CULTURAL AND LITURGICAL BACKGROUND

### The Syriac World in General

In formulating this survey of Syriac theology we are directing our study to that body of thought that grew out of the Syriac culture and language. However, the Syriac world was not homogeneous. It extended from Antioch to Nisibis and the eastern regions. Antioch was a center of Greek culture while possessing a Syriac substratum; Nisibis and the east were embedded in Judeo-Christianity and ancient Persian beliefs.

Sebastian Brock tells us that at the beginning of the Christian era a number of dialects of Aramaic developed of which Syriac was the local dialect of Edessa and its province of Osrhoene. Syriac was to achieve the status of a literary language, since it was adopted as the vehicle for the spread of Christianity in the East.[1]

Robert Murray describes the 'Syriac area' as referring to northern Mesopotamia and Adiabene, the province to the east. He notes that a large number of scholars claim that Edessa was the 'cradle of Syriac Christianity'. Syriac Christianity manifests origins in a thoroughly Jewish form of Christianity, although much Syriac literature contains anti-Jewish writings. He concludes by characterizing the Christianity of Aphraat and Ephrem as a 'breakaway movement among the Jewish community of Adiabene'.[2]

If we look at the Syrian region of the fourth and fifth centuries, we find that while it formed an ethnic and geographic whole, it was divided on a cultural level into two parts. West Syria was bilingual, speaking both Syriac and Greek in its large population centers, and was influenced by hellenistic culture. While Antioch as a center of hellenism had a great influence, the countryside resisted and preserved to a great degree its semetic culture.

East Syria preserved its semetic heritage and resisted Greek influence. In between West and East was the province of Osrohene and its capital, Edessa. The school of Edessa took pride in its Syriac culture, but nevertheless translated into Syriac many of the works of Greek philosophy.[3]

While Plato is found in Syriac chiefly by a number of apocryphal sayings transmitted under his name, much of Aristotle was translated into Syriac, before being translated into Arabic. Porphory is known in Syriac through his introduction to the Organon.[4]

## Aphraat and Ephrem -- heirs of Judeo-Christianity

As we have noted, the authors with which we will deal, such as Aphraat and Ephrem, arose from the milieu of Judeo-Christianity. It was the main influence on their thought. If one looks for specific sources, one can be sure only of the Sacred Scriptures. Robert Murray observes that if Aphraat had one book besides the Bible it was probably a Syriac translation of the Didascalia.[5]

St. Ephrem as an exegete seems to be influenced by a midrashic approach and hermeneutical practice that is Jewish in origin. In dealing with Old Testament themes, he manifests haggadic characteristics. However, he is also a representative of the theoria approach of the Antiochene school of scriptural interpretation.[6] He distinguishes the literal sense from the scriptural.

## The establishment of separate church and liturgical traditions

In various areas of the Christian world, diversity of cultures and customs led to the establishment of various churches. The more highly developed local cultures became the vehicles of sophisticated traditions. In addition, those see cities that claimed to be apostolic and located in large urban centers of civil administration established themselves as seats of ecclesiastical government. It is in these areas that the various patriarchates developed.[7] A similar situation developed in the Syriac region.

R. Taft notes that the East has never known the separation of spirituality, theology, and ecclesiology from liturgy. On the other hand, differences in culture and customs were bound to have an influence on worship. G. Khouri-Sarkis observes that liturgy is the living expression and soul of the people who pray. It is an integrating part of this people, its traditions, its affective needs, whether moral or intellectual.[8]

The Nestorian and Monophysite schisms were also factors in the establishment of the diverse churches and liturgical traditions.

From the point of view of liturgical history, William Macomber has theorized recently that the liturgical situation of the Syriac region around the year 400 was characterized by the presence of at least three rites centered in Antioch, Jerusalem, and Edessa. The first two were in Greek and the last in Syriac. While the Jerusalem rite was limited primarily to Palestine, the rite of Antioch would have been found in the Greek-speaking cities of Syria and as far as Laodicea and Mopsuestia. The rite of Edessa would have been used in the Aramaic-speaking parts of Syria. An interesting development occurred regarding the partisans of Nestorius and the Persian church. While the followers of Nestorius whether in voluntary or forced exile had preached through Mesopotamia and Osrhoene, and in the regions of east and north Syria, it was really the acceptance of the heresy by the school of Edessa where the upper Persian clergy was formed, that led the major part of Mesopotamia and the church of Persia to separate from communion with Constnantinople and constitute the Nestorian church.[9]

Therefore, while adherents to Nestroianism were found in the Greek and Aramaic parts of Syria, they were able to organize themselves ecclesiastically only in the Persian empire. Since the Persian church was highly centralized, the form of the Edessene rite practiced in Iraq soon prevailed for Nestorians everywhere.[10]

W. Macomber describes the Chaldean rite as a product of a fusion of Judeo-Christianity with the Assyro-Babylonian and Iranian cultures. Its liturgical language and its thought categories and imagery were closely akin to those of the Jews of Mesopotamia. Its principal anaphora bore the name of the Apostles Addai and Mari.[11]

Monophysitism in the form of the Jacobite church greatly affected the region and liturgical tradition of Antioch. Among those that rejected Chalcedon were entire provinces of east and west Syria, especially those provinces which spoke Syriac and had not adopted hellenistic culture. There was turmoil in the region for more than a century.[12] As a result, while there was a tendancy to bring uniformity to the rite of Antioch, this desire did not succeed for many centuries. William Macomber speculates that this might explain why some characteristically Maronite features are found in some old liturgical manuscripts of Monophysite origin.[13]

Among the pro-Chalcedonians who were able to preserve their identity in the region of Second Syria were the monks of the monastery of St. Maron near the shores of the Orontes river, and the people who gravitated around them and lived on their lands. These were Aramaic-speaking Chalcedonians who eventually succeeded in organizing an independent hierarchy. Liturgically, according to Macomber, they were able to preserve and develop the ancient Syriac rite of Edessa. In the Maronite tradition, this common anaphora is known as the "Third Anaphora of St. Peter" or "Sharrar". For Macomber elements of this common Edessene rite also appear in other prayers of the Mass, parts of the baptismal rite, and in the hymns of the divine office.[14]

Regarding the liturgical texture of the Syriac region, Macomber concludes that the Syrian rite is basically that of Antioch, but with the anaphoral structure borrowed from the rite of Jerusalem and the metrical hymns either borrowed from or inspired by that of Edessa. The Maronite and Chaldean rites, on the other hand, are in origin independent developments of the ancient Edessene rite. The Maronite rite has subsequently borrowed much from the Syrian rite.[15]

On the political level, the Maronites although surrounded by a monophysite majority affirmed the faith of Chalcedon, propagated it, and defended it with force. Favored and supported by the army of the empire, the Maronites extended their field of action as far as Mesopotamia, Osrhoene, and the Euphratean province. With the Arab invasions, their fortunes changed and so they left Second Syria and sought refuge in the mountains of North Lebanon.[16]

# Notes to the Introduction

1. S. Brock, "Greek into Syriac and Syriac into Greek," Journal of the Syriac Academy (Bagdad), vol. 3 (1977) p. 1.

2. R. Murray, Symbols of Church and Kingdom, (Cambridge: Cambridge University Press, 1975) pp. 5-8.

3. G. Khouri-Sarkis, "Introduction aux Eglises de langue Syriaque," L'Orient Syrien, vol. 1, pp. 7-8.

4. Brock, art. cit., p. 7.

5. Murray, op. cit., p. 337.

6. Tryggve Kronholm, Motifs from Genesis 1-11 in the Genuine Hymns of Ephrem the Syrian, (Uppsala, 1978) pp. 26-27.

7. R. Taft, "The Continuity of Tradition in a World of Liturgical Change: the Eastern Liturgical Experience," Seminarium, vol. 27 (1975) pp. 451-2.

8. Khouri-Sarkis, art. cit., p. 8.

9. Ibid., pp. 8-16.

10. W. Macomber, "A Theory on the Origins of the Syrian, Maronite, and Chaldean Rites," Orientalia Christiana Periodica, vol. 39 (1973) pp. 238-9.

11. W. Macomber, "A History of the Chaldean Mass," Worship, vol. 5 (1977) pp. 107-110.

12. Khouri-Sarkis, art. cit., pp. 16-17.

13. Macomber, "A Theory ..." pp. 239-40.

14. Macomber, "A Theory on the Origins...," pp. 241; Macomber, "A History ...," pp. 110-111. See also: I.H. Dalmais, "L'Heritage Antiochien de l'Église Maronite," Melto, vol. 3, p. 64.

15. Macomber, "A Theory...", p. 242.

16. Khouri-Sarkis, art. cit., pp. 23-25.

# CHAPTER ONE

## THE HIDDENNESS OF GOD

The history of religious experience, in all religious traditions including the Catholic tradition, has been an attempt to affirm the obvious elusiveness of the Holy which is God and yet the conviction that the Divine is within creation and human existence itself. In traditions that believe that God has indeed manifested himself in revelation and exercises an abiding presence in grace, there is sometimes an inclination to act as if this radical distinctness of God from humanity has been overcome. Therefore, an affirmation of the essential mysteriousness of God is also necessary. Such a conviction was a characteristic of the Judaic tradition and was preserved in Judeo-Christianity.

The Syriac Fathers have no doubt of the possession of the life of God in faith and grace. Yet, they are also aware, at the same time, of the abiding mysteriousness and inaccessibility of God. Such is the real paradox at the the heart of Syriac belief. Their Jewish-Christian origins and their familiarity with Scripture engendered a feeling of religious awe. Their world-view presumed an infinite distance between creator and creature, and the ability of the human mind was seen therefore as limited. The long, drawn-out theological controversies of the fourth and fifth centuries raised second-thoughts as to the value of too much "scrutiny" and the feeling that such arguments are eventually counter-productive.

For St. Ephrem (+373), the realm of the divine is radically inaccessible to reason. While the fact of God's existence is knowable, the nature of the divine remains impenetrable. The mysteriousness of God is beyond the grasp also of the angels. Ephrem writes:

...Thousand thousands stand, and ten thousand thousands haste.
The thousands and ten thousands, cannot search out the One:
for all of them stand, in silence and serve.
He has no heir of his throne, save the Son Who is of Him.
In the midst of silence is the enquiry into Him,

1

when the watchers <i.e. angels> come to search
Him out.
They attain to silence and are stayed.[1]

Ephrem explains that only the Son can comprehend
the Father because they are of the same nature. (Hymn
on the Faith, No. 11, 7-11). But this relationship of
connaturality, which is necessary to open our reason to
the divine mystery, is absolutely excluded to all creatures by the radical transcendence of God.

Not having been influenced by the Greek philosophical view of the dichotomy of the soul and body,
Ephrem considers all creatures as composed of basic
elements such as earth, air, fire, and water. He
therefore reasons that corporeal, psychic, and angelic
senses are too gross to perceive the divine. The
spirituality of the human soul or of an angel are the
most subtle forms possible being made up of the two
most pure elements, air and fire. (Hymn on the Faith
No.55, 5). However, since all spiritual creation remains to a certain measure material, the spirituality
of the divine nature is absolute, and transcends radically that of the creature. This is why the divine
nature always remains impenetrable to the spirit and
sense of both angels and men. Ephrem concludes that we
cannot understand the mysteries of nature, of our birth
and death, of our own soul, and so it should not sur-
prise us that we cannot reach the heavens.[2] Ephrem
declares:

If, then, our knowledge cannot even achieve a
knowledge of itself, how does it dare investigate the birth of Him who knows all things?
how can the servant, who does not properly know
himself, pry into the nature of his master?[3]

Ephrem describes, in his Nisibene Hymn, No. 3,
the difficulties of the human mind in searching out
God, and the crucial role played by the Word in the
Incarnation:

Fix thou our hearing, that it be not loosed
and wander! For it is a-wandering if one en-
quire, who He is and what He is like. For how
can we avail, to paint in us the likeness, of
that Being which is like to the mind? Naught
is there in it that is limited, in all of it He
sees and hears; all of it as it were speaks;

2

all of it is in all senses.

Response: Praise to the One Being, that is to us unsearchable!

His aspect cannot be discerned, that it should be portrayed by our understanding... in His graciousness He put on the fashion of humankind and gathered us into His likeness.

...These things were for our profit; that Being in our likeness was made like to us, that we may be made like Him. One there is that is like Him, the Son Who proceeded from Him, Who is stamped with His likeness.[4]

In another passage Ephrem uses the image of the sun and its light. He explains that the eye is too weak to look at the brightness of the sun, and in the same way the divine glory is too strong for his creature. Therefore, it is by the "Son of the Invisible" that we can see the "Invisible". Through his only-begotten Son the invisible essence of the Father is rendered visible. (Hymn on the Faith No. 6)[5]

A favorite image for Ephrem is the pearl which he uses as a symbol of various themes of faith. He also sees it as a parable regarding the immensity of God. In his Hymn on the Pearl, No. 1, he describes the pearl as speaking and referring to itself as the "daughter of the illimitable sea", and because of this bears a wealth of mysteries. While one might search out the sea, one cannot search out the Lord of the sea. Just as divers are able to sustain themselves only for a few moments in the sea, "who would linger and be searching on into the depths of the Godhead?"[6] In various places, Ephrem refers to the Father and Son as two inaccessible seas, and to Divinity as a powerful sea that the human spirit is unable to investigate. The theme of the sea, therefore, is symbolic of a negative theology.[7]

Ephrem takes a middle position regarding the faculty of knowing. He declares that it is not proper to cultivate either ignorance or deep investigation. "For there is One who is perfect in every respect whose knowledge penetratres through all." He cautions that not everything that is clever is true. "...whatever is debated is not deep, but whatever is said by God is subtle when it is believed.'[8]

In his writings, Ephrem is harsh against those whom he calls the "scrutinizers", such as the Arians

3

and others who engaged in endless controversies. It is not only the heresy itself that is at issue, but also the presumption that humans could investigate into the nature of God. Ephrem says in <u>Hymn on the Faith, No. 10</u>:

The strap of your sandal was dread to the discerning;
the hem of your cloak was fearsome to the understanding.
By prying into you, our foolish generation has lost its reason, drunk with new wine.

In fact, R. Murray reasons that Ephrem's answer to intellectual investigation is a symbolical and analogical approach to theology.[9]   A thesis that will be developed in a later chapter.

Ephrem's whole approach to the knowability of God can be expressed in the follwoing passage:

Though your nature is one, its expressions are many;
they find three levels, high, middle, and lowly.
Make me worthy of the lowly part,
of picking up crumbs from the table of your wisdom.
Your highest expression is hidden with your Father,
your middle riches are the wonder of the Watchers.
A tiny stream from your teaching, Lord,
for us below makes a flood of interpretations.[10]

James of Serug (+521) follows the same tradition as Ephrem.   In fact, he uses the imagery of fire to stress the absolute unapproachability of God.   In his <u>Homily No. 94</u>, he describes a "fearful fire" flowing from God.   Therefore, God is far from worshipers and believers, and fearful to those who would wish to seek after Him.   The fire holds back those who would approach God for the purpose of "investigation".[11]

Also, following Ephrem, James points out that the heavenly realities are revealed on the altar of the Eucharist and that one need not desire too far, but can experience heavenly powers in the service of the holy

4

altar. According to R. Chesnut, James does not deal
with the issue of contemplation, nor does he use the
word theoria to describe a mystical ascent of the mind
to God. Reminiscent of the various 'levels' described
by Ephrem, James says:

> In all the heights amongst the crowds he shows
> himself,
> In whatever images he knows that they are able
> to see him.
> To upper beings, in a great thing which is un-
> speakable...
> And to intermediate beings, another crowd, he
> yoked the chariot.
> And he made the Secret descend; he arranged by
> it that his account should come to the world.
> And in the midst of the world, he established
> the altar for bodily creatures,
> And he became a body from whom they should eat,
> their dwelling place. (Homily, No. 125)[12]

According to James of Serug, reason belongs to
the realm of the visible. To use it to try to understand the presence of God in Christ is to engage in
controversy. To try to use Greek philosophy in theology is the work of Satan, who uses it to disturb the
praise that humanity owes to God. Christ "came to enlighten the world, not to be investigated by the world;
he came to save the captives, not to be tracked down by
the saved; he came to make the unclean clean, not that
their mouths make propositions about him."

The only approach to God is through faith and
love, and is granted only to the simple. James writes:

> To love he is near and revealed, and he stands
> like the day;
> But from the controversy of knowers he is
> really far away...
> Oh wise man, (you cannot interpret him)...
> Oh proud scribe, know yourself and see your-
> self.
> And not in pride will you speak the account of
> Immanuel.
> In the simplicity of faith, in perfection, in
> humility speak the account when it is spoken."
> (Homily, No. 40)[13]

The Syriac writer Narsai (+502) was influenced
in his thought by the ideas of Theodore of Mopsuestia,

5

whom he refers to as the 'doctor of doctors'. T. Jansma points out that Ephrem's expositions hardly left a trace in later Nestorian exegetical literature. In fact, even before the time of Narsai, the school of Edessa had adopted the works of Theodore of Mopsuestia in a Syriac translation as the main source of instruction in biblical exegesis. However, when it came to speaking about the inscrutability of God, Narsai works out of the tradition and ideas of Ephrem.[14]

Narsai in his homilies on creation deals with the paradox of the hidden God and the revealed God. On the one hand, he declares that God's being is inaccessible, but he ends by professing the Trinitarian creed. Narsai declares: "The spirit is able only to say: He is and that he is; but to research how he is, the door is closed." For Narsai:

The created is not able to interrogate the Essence of its Author, for as much as he searches how it began, he finds it without beginning.
And for as much as the reflection tries to search his Essence, he discovers only one thing that it is unlimited in nature.
It shall suffice for our inquiry, that we scrutinize only his works, and that the search for his Essence is honored by us in silence.[15]

Nevertheless, Narsai attempts to enumerate the properties of God. Using negative language, he describes God as non-corporeal, infinite, invisible, and immutable. Later in his writings, Narsai even lists positive Divine attributes: God is omnipresent, omnipotent, omniscient, and prescient. However, he concludes his effort by saying that God cannot be understood, the research is indefinite. Since God is without limits, the research fatigues man: "Leave, searcher, do not tire yourself studying what is hidden. Know your nature and give glory to Him who constituted it."[16]

God is manifest by his revelation and can only be sought out in faith and by love as embodied in contemplative prayer. Narsai declares: "Let us search by faith alone, in order that we believe, although it also is not obtained by the search, but by love. By love, it is possible for us to search the hidden, how it is, and how there are three equal Persons.[17]

6

In another place, Narsai advises that the searcher should search as is proper when seeking the One who is without limit, but is one nature and three Persons. Therefore, the search is limited to studying Paternity, Filiation, and Procession. Nevertheless, even in this, one achieves understanding not by the search but by love. Only contemplation done without curiosity is good.[18]

T. Jansma offers a good summary of the views of both Ephrem and Narsai regarding the knowability of God. According to these two Syriac fathers, the Being of the Maker is beyond space and time; it is concealed, hidden, incomprehensible, inscrutable, infinite. Created beings are not capable of understanding God, and err in trying to scrutinize, investigate and search into God's Being. So humans should try to know their own nature and not weary themselves by scrutinizing, but marvel and be struck with awe; they must accept the inscrutable with love and faith, and honor it in silence.[19]

The Maronite liturgy reflects both in the Service of the Holy Mysteries and the Divine Office the idea of the hiddenness of God. For example, the 'prayer of forgiveness' or 'hoosoyo' for Pentecost begins with the salutation: "May we be worthy to praise, confess, and glorify the Mystical One, who is hidden from human thought, understanding and perfection..."[20]

An example from the Divine Office is the 'prayer of forgiveness' for the fourth "qawmo" of Lilyo (the night office), which states in its salutation: "...to the One who, from the beginning is the unique and true God, and who eternally transcends all faculty, intelligence and human thought, for he is inexplicable, incomprehensible, and ungraspable; who alone knows himself..."[21]

## God as Light

While the chapter on revelation will deal with God's revealing of himself through his Word, one of the more basic images associated with God is the theme of light. It may be rooted in the primoridal light described in Genesis, or the universal symbol of light representing goodness, while darknesses symbolizes chaos and evil. Christ is described in terms of light especially in his Baptism at the Jordan, his cross is seen exalted as a cross of light and a lighthouse. The light which is Christ shatters the darkness of 'sheol', and the shining face of the Father and/or Christ is the hope of the deceased. This theme of light coincides perhaps with the vision of God as light in various mystical traditions.

Ephrem in his <u>Hymn of the Church No. 36</u> says:

Give thanks to the Creator of the light
wherein is depicted
the heavenly Light;
give praise to the Maker of the light
that is a symbol
of the Light of our Savior!

In the same hymn he applies this theme to Christ in this way:

Just as Moses gleamed
with the divine glory
because he saw the splendor briefly
how much more should the body
wherein Christ resided gleam,
and the river where he was baptized?[22]

The Syriac liturgies celebrate the theme of light often. In the Chaldean liturgy, the long office of "sapra" (dawn) prays: "Creator of the light, enlighten us by your light, rejoice us by your coming, ...joyous and renewing Light." By Christ, the reflection of the substance of God, "we are lead into light; illumined by his joyous light", we await the full light which shall shine in the 'parousia'.[23]

The various meanings of the theme of light are celebrated often in the Maronite liturgy. The prayer for light in the Divine Office of Saturday morning states:

O Lord God, be a perpetual morning for us, a light which does not fade and a day that does not end. Then we shall be illumined by the light of your holy commandments in our feelings, thoughts, and desires. Our Lord and our God, glory to you forever.

The eschatological theme of the light that will not end is seen in the prayer of conclusion of the common for evening prayer:

8

...By your will, Lord, you have made the day to cease and the night to come, and it is by your order that night reigns; be for us that great day that does not pass away! At twilight, make your light to shine in our hearts and in the darkness of night enlighten us by the knowledge of your truth...

The theme of light is specifically applied to the God-man. The "sedro" (i.e. the body of the prayer of forgivenss) in the morning office of Christmas contains the following ideas: "Son of our God, Word and Image of the Father,... Your light is more resplendent than light, your sun more brilliant than the sun, and your day more magnificent than the day..."

The salvific effect of the Light and the image of the 'face of Christ' as light can be seen in the opening prayer of the Service of the Holy Mysteries for the first three weeks of Lent: "O Lord God, enlighten our hearts and consciences with the radiance of Your face that we may walk in the rays of Your light during this season of Lent..."

# Notes to Chapter One

1. St. Ephrem, "Hymn on the Nativity, No. 14,", Nicene and Post-Nicene Fathers, Second Series, transl. by A. Edward Johnston, (Grand Rapids: Wm Eerdmans Publishing Company, 1964) vol. 13, pp. 251-2.

2. A. de Halleux, "Mar Ephrem Theologien," Parole de l'Orient, vol. 4 (1973) pp. 43-44.

3. St. Ephrem, "Hymn on the Faith, No. 1," Harp of the Spirit, transl. by Sebastian Brock, (Fellowship of St. Alban and St. Sergius, 1975) p. 7.

4. St. Ephrem, "Nisibene Hymn, No. 13", Nicene and Post-Nicene Fathers, transl. by J.T. Stopford, pp. 170-1.

5. G. Saber, La Théologie Baptismale de Saint Ephrem (Kaslik: Université de Saint-Esprit, 1974) p. 28.

6. St. Ephrem, "Hymn on the Pearl, No. 1", Nicene and Post-Nicene Fathers, transl by J.B. Morris, p. 293.

7. P. Yousif, "Symbolisme Christologique dans la Bible et dans la Nature chez S. Ephrem de Nisibe," Parole de l'Orient, vol. 8 (1977-8) p 24.

8. T. Jansma, "Ephraem on Exodus II, 5: Reflections on the Interplay of Free will and Divine Providence," Orientalia Christiana Periodica, vol. 39 (1973) p. 17.

9. Robert Murray, "A Hymn of St. Ephrem to Christ on the Incarnation, the Holy Spirit, and the Sacraments," Eastern Churches Review, vol. 3 (1970-71) pp. 144, 149.

10. Ibid., p. 143.

11. Roberta Chesnut, Three Monophysite Christologies: Severus of Antioch, Philoxenus of Mabbug, and Jacob of Sarug, (London: Oxford University Press, 1976) p. 138.

12. Ibid., p. 139.

13. Ibid., pp. 140-41.

14. T. Jansma, "Narsai and Ephraem: Some observations on Narsai's Homelies on Creation and Ephraem's Hymns on

Faith," Parole de l'Orient, vol. 1 (1970) pp. 49-50.

15. Ibid., p. 54.

16. T. Jansma, "Études sur la Pensée de Narsai," L'Orient Syrien, vol. 11 (1966) p. 151.

17. Jansma, "Narsai and Ephraem...," p. 53.

18. P. Gignoux, "Homélie de Narsai sur le Mot 'Au Commencement" et sur l'essence Divine," L'Orient Syrien, vol. 8 (1963) p. 233.

19. Jansma, "Narsai and Ephraem...," p. 60

20. Citations from the Maronite liturgy, unless indicated otherwise, are taken from: Lectionary, Syriac-Maronite Church, The Seasons (Detroit: Diocese of St. Maron--U.S.A, 1976); Anaphora Book of the Syriac Maronite Church of Antioch (Youngstown: Diocese of St. Maron, 1978); Fenqitho, A Treasury of Feasts According to the Syriac-Maronite Church of Antioch (Diocese of St. Maron, 1980).

21. Cited by Jean Tabet, L'Office Commun Maronite: Étude du Lilyo et du Safro, (Kaslik, Universite de Saint-Esprit, 1972) p. 145.

22. Sebastian Brock, "St. Ephrem on Christ as Light in Mary and in the Jordan: Hymni de Ecclesia 36," Eastern Churches Review, vol. 7 (1975) pp. 138-39.

23. Pierre-Thomas Camelot, "Lumière," Dictionnaire de Spiritualité, vol. 9, cols. 1154-5.

# CHAPTER TWO

## CREATION AND SIN

The Syriac view of creation is more a product of Biblical influence and faith experience, than philosophical speculation. Moreover, creation, revelation, and Incarnation are viewed as elements of one divine process. Therefore, creation cannot be separated from God's self-revelation or from the event of the Word becoming creature. In the next chapter, we will discuss the view of the Syriac writers that creation is in its very nature revelatory through types and symbols. The present chapter deals with the creation of the world and humanity. In this regard, we will note that the Syriac writers claimed that the Biblical declaration that humans are created in the image and likeness of God, refers to their being the reflection of the pre-existent Christ. Another significant insight is that humanity itself is understood as the converging point of creation.

### The pre-existence of Christ

St. Ephrem, in his Commentary on Genesis, interprets the verse, "Let us create man in our image" (Gen. 1,26), as a mysterious revelation of God's First-Born (Christ), the Image of God, in his creating and redeeming activity. For Ephrem, every command regarding creation in the beginning was directed to Christ who is God's 'Voice'. In the Hymn on the Faith, No. 6, Ephrem states:

> In the Beginning, however, the works have been created through the First-Born. For (It is written:) God said: "Let there be light -- and it was created." Whom, now did he command, when there was nothing? Fully revealed is the truth to him who wants to see it: the six days that were created give testimony... that (the Creator) did not give commands to the (created) works that they should make themselves. Nay, through the One from the One were they created. The Father commanded through his Voice, the Son carried out the work.

Ephrem then concludes:

> ...In the creation of man, finally, the

13

Omniscient took heed...to reveal his First-Born abundantly.[1]

Therefore, the key phrase, "Let us make man in our image, after our likeness," is making a fundamental affirmation that the Word of God is in the image of God and that God's relationship with humans is realized by the mediation of the Word. While Christ as the Word is the image of the Father, he is also the perfect figure of man. Humanity finds its perfect realization in Christ.[2]

Regarding salvation-history, Ephrem speculates that the divine love that created humans through Christ out of love would foresee the rejection by man and his wandering astray, and his restoration. In the Nisibene Hymn, No. 69, he states:

> You have formed the dust from the beginning, in mercy, and you are to bring your gift towards it to completion, in love. You, O Good One, have created man. Although it was obvious to you, that he would reject you and go astray, you formed him, in order to justify him (when he had fallen).[3]

James of Serug also affirms that humanity in the person of the 'great Adam' had originally been created by God the Father in the image of his Son as he was to appear on earth, that is, in the image of Jesus. In Homily 125, he declares:

> Before the created things, the Father sealed the image of his Son, and formed him and showed him how he would shine among earthly beings. The Father looked at the image of his Son and formed Adam...[4]

Narsai supports the view that the model for creation is Christ. In his Homily No. 62, he explains:

> He (the Creator) called the first Adam by the name of image in a secondary sense. The image in reality is the Messiah, the second Adam. Thus 'Come let us make man in our image' was fulfilled when the Creator took His image and made it a dwelling place for His honor. The promises to Adam came to be in reality in the Messiah.[5]

14

The Maronite liturgy reflects the role of the Word in creation. The Preface of the Anaphora of James of Serug declares: "King of the Ages, and Inscrutable Hiddenness, Your beloved Son is being from your being, the appearance of your light, and the reflection of your glory. He is the power of your Word, through whom You created the world..." A similar thought is expressed in the Preface of the Anaphora of John Maron: "Father, unsearchable Lord of all generations, You sent the Lord Jesus, who is equal to You. As your Word, He is the brightness of your fire, and the image of your all-powerful being. Through Him You created the generations in your grace..."

## Creation of humanity in the image and likeness of God

Humans are the highest work of creation, since they are made in the image of God's First-Born. Reflecting Genesis, Ephrem understands the soul of Adam as having been engendered by God's own breath. This means that humans therefore possess the singular faculties of speech and freedom. Ephrem states:

> For when the hand of the Creator had formed the body, and constructed it, in order that it should sing to its Maker, there was no sound in the silent harp, until he breathed into it at last the soul that sang through it, so that its strings got sound and even (the soul) through its agency got the ability to express wisdom. (Hymn on Paradise, no. 8)[6]

In fact, Ephrem understands free-will as the quality by which Adam was the image of God.[7] By their capacity of free decision, humans are like God. Commenting on Genesis, Ephrem presents God as saying: "Let us make man in our image; that is to say that he has the power to listen to us, if he will listen to us."[8]

Ephrem stresses the significance of human freedom in the Hymn on the Epiphany, No. 10:

> ...the compulsion of God is an all-prevailing force;
> (but that is not pleasing to Him which is of compulsion)
> as that which is of discerning will
> therefore in our fruits He calls us
> who live not as under compulsion, by persuasion.

Good is He, for lo! He labors in these
two things;
He wills not to constrain our freedom
nor again does He suffer us to abuse it.
For had he constrained it, He had taken away
its power,
and had He let it go, He had deprived it of
help.

He knows that if He constrains He de-
prives us;
He knows that if He casts off He destroys us;
He knows that if He teaches He wins us.
He has not constrained and He has not cast off,
as the Evil One does:
He has taught, chastened, and won us, as being
the good God.[9]

In the Hymn of Faith, No. 25, Ephrem summarizes
his position poetically:

Because you are a harp endowed of life and
language, says he, your chords and words possess liberty. O harp, who of itself and according to its own will chants of its God.[10]

Aphraat develops his own theological anthropology based on an understanding that human beings
are composed of body, soul, and spirit, and reflecting
the Biblical teaching that God breathed his spirit into
humans. There are times when Aphraat seems to be
saying that it is God's very spirit that humans possess
and thus have life. It is God, the living One, who
gives life through his spirit. Aphraat speculates that
it is the Spirit of God that becomes the prophetic
spirit that speaks to Ezechial; that lived in Saul
after his royal anointing, but was later lost; and that
also inhabited David but not in continuous fashion.
This spirit has been found during the course of the
history of Israel as a spirit of knowledge and wisdom.

Christ received the Spirit in fulness at this
Baptism, and thereby freely received his messianic consecration. By baptism we put on the spirit of Christ.
Before baptism humans have only "animal spirit" which
they receive by creation, but in the second birth, they
receive the holy spirit of God.

Humans are created with a living soul (that is,

16

the life principle) and are destined to become "living spirit". Thanks to the intervention of the spirit, the good become 'spiritual', incorruptible and immortal, while the evil are not transformed but remain in the dust in which Adam was created, in the "animal condition".[11]

F.C. Burkitt summarizes this doctrine of Aphraat as follows:

Such is the creed of Aphraates. To him Christianity was the revelation of a Divine Spirit dwelling in man and fighting against moral evil, not first and foremost a tissue of philosophical speculation about the nature of Divinity itself.[12]

The fact that humans are created in the image and likeness of God has moral consequences. Aphraat in his Homily on Admonition and Repentance reasons:

...If you should insult the King's image, you shall pay the penalty of murder; and if you revile a man, you revile the image of God.

...You have a spiritual nature; the soul is the image of the Creator; honor the image of God, by being in agreement with all men.[13]

Narsai adds that it is the whole human person and not only the soul that is in the image of God. In Homily No. 66, he declares: "The creator willed to call it (the soul) and the body His image."[14]

James of Serug concludes that humanity was created originally as a kind of double image -- as an image of the Son, who is the image of the Father, but also as an image of the Son made man. The humanity of Christ, then, is in a primordial relationship to the human race. Adam is in a very special sense the image of God. In Homily 94 he explains:

The image of the Son, the only one, he gave to Adam, while he was its creator, he took it from him when he visited him... While he was its creator, he was related to him who gave him the image... To his own he came; in his image he dwelt in the daughter of Adam, who was formed in his image, and because of this he was related to him.[15]

17

## Humans as the converging point of creation

Syriac anthropology arrives at the conclusion that humans are not only the summit of creation, but also the bond uniting the heavens and the earth. The body of Adam was formed of dust from the earth in its virginal state to become a true microcosm. In fact, Ephrem sees in the way of Adam's creation and the purpose of his creation, a type of the conception of Christ, the New Adam and reconciler of the world, born in the virginal womb of Mary.[16] Being in the image of God who has power over all things high and low, Adam also has power over all creation.[17]

Narsai stresses this theme in his Homily No. 66:

He (the Creator) fashioned and skilfully made a double vessel, a visible body and a hidden soul -- one man. He depicted the power of His creatorship in him as an image: mute beings in his body and rational beings in the structure of his soul.[18]

Therefore, by the life of the soul he is linked to the angels, and by the structure of the body, he draws near to corporeal beings.

Narsai goes further and sees humans in a role of mediation between creatures and God. In Homily No. 62, he presents God as saying: "I set him like an image for creatures, so that they might consider him in order that by love to him everyone might know me."[19]

The Syriac mystic, Simon of Taibutheh, embodies this theological view with a spiritual admonition:

Consider, O discerning man, that you are the image of God and the bond of all creation, both of the heavenly and of the terrestrial beings, and whenever you bend your head to worship and glorify God, all the creations, both heavenly and terrestrial, bow their heads with you and in you, to worship God; and whenever you do not worship and glorify Him, all the creatures grieve over you and turn against you, and you fall from grace.[20]

## Grace as the 'robe of glory'

In his theological anthropology, Ephrem

18

expresses the teaching on grace with the image of 'robe of glory'. He understands Christ as vested in this robe from the beginning. He also uses this image regarding Adam. Jewish legend had it that Adam and Eve had been clothed in paradise but lost it at the Fall. Isaiah 61, 3 refers to it as a mantle of praise.[21] Ephrem describes humans before the Fall as endowed with a particular "glory" which was subsequently lost, but restored through baptism.[22]

In his Commentary on the Gospel (Arm.) 19, 17, Ephrem explains:

For in the same way that he created by grace the first essence of creatures so that they were without stain, in the glory and magnificence that he had clothed himself, so by the mercy of God, there would be a new creation of all things, without stain, in the glory that he was clothed again.[23]

James of Serug declares:"The robe of glory that was stolen away among the trees of Paradise have I put on in the waters of baptism."[24]

## Conscience and Sin

For Ephrem and his colleagues, human virtue consists in studying the law of God and internalizing it in one's heart and conscience. In his Letter to Publius, Ephrem demonstrates a rather sophisticated understanding of the interplay of law and conscience in guiding human freedom:

My opinion is that this inner intelligence has been made the judge and the law, for it is the embodiment of the shadow of the law, and it is the shadow of the Lord of the law... <It teaches> all yet using no force, giving counsel, but employing no compulsion reminding them of the judgement to come by means of warnings, bringing to their mind the kingdom of heaven so that they may desire it, explaining the rewards of the good so that they may yearn for them, showing to them the power of judgement, that they may restrain themselves, telling them of the gentleness of the Only-begotten, that they may take courage, running with them after every good thing and strengthening them, hovering over them and rebuking them as they stoop to what is hateful... Here <on earth> it is mingled with them in every way, while there it stands up in front of them in this day <of judgement>.[25]

Sin for the Syriac fathers is due to error and darkness which results in a loss of freedom. It consists ultimately in a distortion of the image of God that human beings are, and in a loss of the harmony between the heavens and the earth.

The Maronite divine office reflects this thinking. In the "sedro" (prayer of forgiveness) of the morning office of Tuesday it prays:

Be blessed and honored, O Lord who has created light, dissipated and annihilated darkness; you have delivered us from the sleep of error and have granted us morning for our joy and to make us see the light of your creative power and the sublime grandeur of your wisdom...

The same theme is repeated in the "sedro" of the evening office of Tuesday which declares:

...Accept our vigil, be favorable to our service, that your calm reign in us and your peace guide our hearts; so that darkness would not be in our spirit and it not be prey to the obscurity of sin...

Developing another theme, the first prayer of the morning office of the Monday of Holy Week prays: "Son of the Father, you have taken the condition of a slave and have become for us a curse to restore to us lost freedom..."

James of Serug discusses the theological impact of original sin on our being the image of God and on the harmony of creation. For James, Adam and Eve had been placed in paradise to be gardeners. However, in the first contest with the 'Great Dragon' <James' image for Satan>, Adam was defeated, and a "wall of enmity" was established between God and the human race, "the upper beings and the lower beings". Cast out of Eden, Adam, "the Great Image", lay corrupting in sheol, separated from the "Hidden Father" by a seemingly insurmountable barrier.[26] In the divine liturgy, the prayer after the Preface of the Anaphora of John the Evan-

gelist declares:    "...You sent Your Son who became man
and suffered for us who distorted the image in which we
were created."

The same world-view is echoed later in Theodore
of Mopsuestia and Cyrus of Edessa. One theory of creation was that the world was created in an original harmony that was broken by Adam's disobedience, and has
been restored by Christ's obedience. According to
Theodore, God intended that the universe should be, as
it were, a simple body, united in the service of praise
of Himself. However, since the universe consists of
two parts with opposed charcteristics, the spiritual
creation of immaterial and invisible natures, and the
corporeal creation of material and sensible natures,
there was need of a bond to unite the two contrasting
parts into a single harmonious whole. This bond was
humanity, in whom the spiritual and corporeal are
united in a single nature. Cyrus refers to humans as
"creation's containing vessel". Adam's sin of disobedience, by introducing death into human nature, dis-
rupted the union of spirit and matter, first of all and
directly in himself and his descendents, but secondly
and indirectly in all of creation[27]

The vision of creation and the role of humans
presented in this chapter can be summarized best in a
hymn of thanksgiving composed by St. Ephrem in his Commentary on the Diatesseron:

We adore you, who have sent us into the
world, who has given us rule over all that is
there, and withdraws it in an hour that we do
not know... The earth praises you, who open
her womb and give her fruits in season. The
oceans praise you by the mouth of their waves,
when their voices proclaim that you rule them.
The trees praise you, when they are constrained
by the breath of the wind to weep and give
fruits. They bless you also, the plants so
varied and the multicolored flowers... May
they be gathered and unite their voice in your
praise, in gratitude for all your goods and
united in peace to bless you; that all co-
operate to build a work of praise.[28]

21

# Notes to Chapter Two

1. T. Kronholm, Motifs from Genesis 1-11, pp. 40-41.

2. Nabil El-khoury, "Gen. 1, 26 -- Dans l'Interprétation de Saint Ephrem, Ou La Relation de l'Homme À Dieu," Orientalia Christiana Analecta, vol. 205 (1978) pp. 199-200.

3. Kronholm, op. cit., p. 50.

4. Cited by R. Chesnut, Three Monophysite Christologies, pp. 113-4. See also: E. Khalifé-hachem, "Homélie Metrique de Jacques de Saroug sur l'amour," Parole de l'Orient, vol. 1, 286.

5. Cited by Frederick McLeod, "Man as the Image of God: its meaning and theological signficance in Narsai," Theological Studies, vol. 42 (1981) p. 462.

6. Cited by Kronholm, op. cit., p. 58.

7. See: T. Jansma, "Ephraem on Exodus II, 5: Reflections on the Interplay of Human Free Will and Divine Providence," Orientalia Christiana Periodica, vol. 39 (1973) p. 18.

8. El-Khoury, art. cit., p. 199.

9. Nicene and Post-Nicene Fathers, p. 281.

10. El-Khoury, art. cit., p. 203.

11. R. Terzoli, "Ame et Esprit chez Aphraate," Parole de l'Orient, vol. 3 (1972) pp. 108-13.

12. F.C. Burkitt, Early Eastern Christianity, (London, 1904) p. 85.

13. Nicene and Post-Nicene Fathers, pp. 330-1. See also: Khalife-hachem, art. cit., p. 289.

14. Cited by McLeod, art. cit., p. 459.

15. Cited by Chesnut, op. cit., p. 127.

16. Kronholm, op. cit., p. 45.

17. El-Khoury, art. cit., p. 199.

18. Cited by McLeod, art. cit., pp. 460-1. See also: P. Gignoux, "Homélie de Narsai sur la Creation du Monde," L'Orient Syrien, vol. 7 (1962) p. 480; and T. Jansma, "Narsai and Ephraem: Some observations on Narsai's Homelies on Creation and Ephraem's Hymns on the Faith," Parole de l'Orient, vol. 1 (1970) p. 51.

19. Cited by McLeod, art. cit., p. 462.

20. "Mystical Works of Simon of Taibuteh," Woodbrooke Studies, transl. by A, Mingana, (Cambridge: W. Heffer and Sons, Ltd., 1934) vol. 7, p. 8.

21. See: S. Brock, "Word and Sacrament in the Writings of the Syrian Fathers," Sobornost, vol. 6.10 (1974) pp. 689-70.

22. Kronholm, op. cit., p. 62.

23. El-Khoury, art. cit., p. 202.

24. Brock, art. cit., pp. 689-70.

25. S. Brock, "Ephrem's Letter to Publius," Le Museon, vol. 89 (1976) pp. 292-3.

26. Chesnut, op. cit., pp. 113-4.

27. W.F. Macomber, "The Theological Synthesis of Cyrus of Edessa, an East Syrian Theologian of the Mid-Sixth Century," Orientalia Christiana Periodica, vol. 30 (1964) pp. 9-17.

28. El-Khoury, art. cit., pp. 204-5.

# CHAPTER THREE

## REVELATION

As we have seen, the Syriac mind was in awe of the radical inaccessiblity and mysteriousness of God. Only the Word of God expresses God and would possibly manifest God. However, any attempt to understand the Word taking on created form would necessarily involve paradox and dialectic. Ephrem has been described as moving between apophatic and cataphatic poles. On the one hand, there is God's absolute transcendence, and the incommunicability of his name to humans. On the other hand, human terms are inapplicable to Him. Ephrem in his Commentary on the Diatesseron points out: "Among the ancients wisdom was recognized more in works than in words, and to the use of the tongue they preferred the power of the mind reflecting in silence."[1] In the Ephremic dialectic, the moment of revelation follows normally that of lack of understanding.[2]

It was Ephrem's conviction that creation itself is revelatory. In this context, he speaks of nature, the Old Testament, and the New Testament as sources of revelation. According to A. de Halleux Ephrem considers revelation as a process engaging God himself in a sort of progressive incarnation. In imprinting in nature and Sacred Scripture the signs which reveal him, it is as if God were preparing to put on the human body of Jesus. God goes out from eternal simplicity to enter the multiplicity of history. It is in this sense that Ephrem speaks of the 'changings' that God, by nature immutable, has appropriated by love. Immeasurable in himself, he has manifested himself in creation and in the Incarnation, and finally in the miracles, all of which reveal to us only a faint ray of his glory. These 'changings' of God do not concern his immutable nature but his divine will, demonstrating its power and its goodness.[3]

Ephrem understands creation as revelatory because it was created by the Word himself. He says: "Where you look, the symbol of Christ is present. And where you read, you find his types. For it is by him that all creatures have been made, and he has marked all his works by his symbols, since he created the world." (Hymn on Virginity, 20, 2).[4] Ephrem sees the world as a symbolic whole. The world of terrestrial realities not only signifies, but pre-contains, in some

25

ways, celestial realities. Images, words, and names in particular, retain something of the essence of the beings that they signify. The universe is an immense Christological symbol, having for its end to reveal the Son of God and to prepare humanity for his coming. Ephrem declares:

> Creatures trace the symbols of Christ. Mary has formed the members of his body, but many wombs have given birth to the Unique Son; the womb of his mother gave birth to his humanity, but creatures have given birth to him symbolically. (Hymn on Virginity 6, 7-8)[5]

The elements of matter are for Ephrem visual means which express the work of God. (Hymn on Virginity, 11) Ephrem, enlightened by faith, sees in nature a symbol which speaks of God, of his works and his mysteries, for God has left traces in the universe. (Unleavend Bread, 4, 24; On Virginity, 8, 2; 20, 12)[6]

Robert Murray summarizes this viewpoint by pointing out that Ephrem's poetical-theological method beyond his use of types, symbols, and even sacramental "mysteries" is based on a grand conception of the harmony between God and all the orders of creation. God has filled creation with his traces, and has given humans the mind and the faculty of language which can appreciate these pointers, express them, and follow them by the light of the gift of faith.[7]

Sebastian Brock believes that Ephrem is a representative of a Christian view that God and the "holy" is immanent in the world. Therefore, Ephrem sees connections between everything in creation as possible pointers to Christ. All that is required is the eye of faith. To express these relationships Ephrem resorts to typology, and other literary forms such as parallelism and paradox. Brock goes so far as to claim that types and symbols are not simply pointers, but for Ephrem the symbol contains within itself the actual presence of that which it symbolizes. Thus, Ephrem has a sacramental view of the world.[8] In Ephrem's own words: "Because of the visible type you are able to see invisible realities with the eye." (Hymn of Faith No. 87, 3)[9]

For Ephrem, it is ultimately the Incarnation and the Mysteries (i.e. sacraments) that make it possible for humans to cope with the divine. On the one hand,

26

the body of Christ serves as a necessary shield so that divinity can be revealed to us. In his Homily on Nativity, Ephrem explains:

The face of Moses shone
when God spoke with him,
and he laid a veil over his face
for the people were unable to behold him
--just as our Lord, from the womb,
entered and put on the veil of the body;
He shone out and went forth, and the Magi
beheld Him and brought gifts.[10]

This motif is reflected in the Maronite liturgy. For example, the prayer of forgiveness for Holy Thursday states: "O Lord Jesus Christ, God the Word, You are the Lord of heavenly and earthly creatures and the consuming Flame which the fiery ranks of heaven dare not look upon. In your compassion, you clothed yourself with a body. The heavenly creatures who serve You with reverence hide their faces before you..."

However, Christ is not only a shield of the awesome essence of God, but also the most appropriate vehicle of revelation. Ephrem observes:

The eye is too weak to fix on the great brightness of the sun. Without the Son of the Invisible, the eye would not know how to see the Invisible. His glory is too strong for his creature. By his unique Son, the Invisible Essence renders itself visible and expresses itself by symbols. By bread we eat the strength which is not consummable, by wine we drink the fire that is not quenchable, and by oil we are anointed by a power that cannot be diminished. As he made himself tender for the mouth to take pleasure and eat, he has softened his appearance for the eyes and his might in words, that the ear might hear him. (Hymn on the Faith No. 6, 2-4)[11]

However, according to Ephrem, God's revelation has a dialectical character. In his very revelation, God remains the hidden God. His images hide as much as they manifest. The more he appears close, the more he remains far. Expressing the presence of divine transcendence within creation presents a problem, in the absence of philosophical categories. As we shall see in the next section, Ephrem's solution is found in his

27

use of paradox, for example, to express power in weakness as seen in his writings on the Nativity and the Passion[12], and in his use type and symbol.

Furthermore, Ephrem holds the view that revelation and even Incarnation can be only partially successful in manifesting the mysteriousness of God. He declares:

> If someone concentrate his attention solely
> on the metaphors used of God's majesty,
> he abuses and misrepresents that majesty
> by means of those metaphors with which God has
> clothed himself for man's own benefit,
> and he is grateful to that Grace
> which bent down its stature to the level of
> man's childishness:
> although God had nothing in common with it,
> He clothed himself in the likeness of man
> in order to bring man to the likeness of himself.
> Do not let your intellect be disturbed by mere names,
> for Paradise has simply clothed itself in terms
> that are familiar to you:
> it is not because it is poor that it has put on
> your imagery,
> rather, your nature is far too weak to be able
> to attain to its greatness, and its beauties
> are much diminished
> by being depicted in the pale colors that you
> are familiar with. (Hymns on Paradise 11, 6-7) [13]

## Types, symbols, and paradox

For Ephrem the principal way that the mystery of God's manifestation in creation can be expressed is in type, symbol, and mystery. He uses the Syriac term "raza" to express these ideas. P. Yousif claims that Ephrem understands the term "raza" in four senses: enigma, as in the original Persian where it meant royal secrets, as found in the Aramaic of Daniel 6, 4, where it means divine secrets (see On the Unleavened Bread 14, 11); mystery, that is, a reality which surpasses human intelligence (for example, On the Crucifixion 8, 5, regarding the being of Christ); a simple sign, that is, a means of knowledge and of indication, such as the symbols of nature which proclaim Christ (see Hymn on the Faith, No. 18); and symbol-mystery, that is, ele-

28

ments of the Old Testament become the reality of the New Testament, also, to signify the divine realities of the Church, for example, the sacraments.[14]

Robert Murray explains that Ephrem's vision depended on the belief that all the Old Testament pointed to Christ. "Raza" or mystery became the word for the 'Christ-bearing' sense concealed in Old Testament figures conveying the idea of type and anti-type. Christ being the fulfillment is the 'truth' or 'reality'. The Bible contains revelatory symbols of Christ, because creation does. Murray observes that the reason so many trees or pieces of wood in the Old Testament can be seen as types of the Cross is that the eye of faith sees every tree as pregnant with the mystery of the Cross.[15] This last meaning will be discussed in a later chapter.

Ephrem states clearly that the method by which nature reveals Christ is by type and symbol. He explains in his Hymn on Virginity No. 5:

In the Garden of Eden and the terrestrial world
our Lord's symbols multiply themselves.
Who can gather in all the pictures of his mystery?
In each one of them Christ is depicted in full.
Things visible await you, Lord; types seek you
out, the symbols prefigure you,
parables take their refuge in you.[16]

However, Ephrem continues to caution that even in symbol God remains hidden:

However much, Lord, I would feel You, it is
still not You yourself I touch,
for my mind can touch nothing of Your hiddenness:
it is just a visible, illumined, image
that I see in the symbol of You; for all investigation into Your being is hidden. (Nisibene Hymn, No. 50)[17]

This viewpoint of types foreshadowing Christ continued in Syriac tradion. For example, Philoxenus of Mabboug, who follows a typological interpretation in dealing with Scripture, teaches that God the Father is mysterious, but is the "archtype" who manifests himself in types and shadows until the full revelation occurs in the Word made flesh. Types and mysteries of Christ

29

were formed and inscribed in the Old Testament.[18]

Perhaps the most striking literary form used by Ephrem and the Syriac fathers is paradox. In this approach, God's mysteriousness is preserved while events from human experience are juxtaposed antithetically as vehicles of meaning. Paradox is the imagination's counterpart to the intellect's use of the principle of analogy. It is one way in which human speech can embody divine realities. For example, Ephrem in his _Hymn on the Nativity_, No. 118 declares:

The Mighty One entered and put on insecurity
from Mary's womb; the Provisioner of all entered -- and experienced hunger;
He who gives drink to all entered
-- and experienced thirst;
naked and stripped
there came forth from Mary He who clothes all.[19]

James of Serug uses the same method in his homilies:

You yourself remain in grandeur and in smallness, and that is why anyone who wishes to speak trembles before you. If he tries to speak of your simpleness he perceives your overwhelming grandeur, contemplates it, and is stopped. And when he wishes to speak of your grandeur, he is embarrassed, seeing the sufferings and the abasement which happened to you.

...A sight without precedent, a young virgin giving of her milk; a great marvel, a death from which hurls forth life. The orator trembles from beginning to end, since the whole route is full of marvels which he contemplates. Seeing your sufferings, one thinks you are a man, seeing the prodigies and marvels, one knows that you are a God.[20]

The Maronite liturgy is filled with instances of paradox. The verse before the Scripture readings for Wednesday chants: "It is fitting to remember the Holy Virgin Mary because she carried in her womb God, who sustains the universe." The Evening Prayer of the divine office for Palm Sunday contains the following verse before the Scripture readings: "He who rides on the clouds, rides today on an ass; he who the earth and the heavens bless, is blessed today by the mouths of children." And, the verse before the Scripture readings of Morning Prayer declares: "Today in Jerusalem children surround him whom the powers of light surround in heaven." The 'prayer of forgiveness' for the Morning Office of Good Friday prays:

Incarnate Word, Son of Mary and Son of the Father, on this day, the greatest in all history, you were brought to trial scornfully before Pilate, you who are seated in glory at the right of your Father. You remain silent before your judges, but by it, you speak all things. You walk on the road to Golgotha carrying the wood of the cross, you who are seated on the throne of cherubim clothed in luminous raiment. On your head, the thorns are wreathed in a crown of derision, you whose head the heavens adorn with a crown of stars. On the cross you are given to drink of vinegar and gall, you who give us to drink your blood. Source of life, you die on the wood of the cross, you who do not cease to give life to all the living on earth...

## Christ in nature, and in the Old and New Testaments

As we have noted above, Ephrem describes God the Father and Christ playing on two or three harps in manifesting themselves, namely, nature, and the Old and New Testaments. In his Hymn on Virginity, No. 29, he speaks of the Word putting on a body, and with his hands playing two harps. He places a third harp before his face as a witness for the other two.[21]

In the Hymn on Virginity, No. 28, Ephrem combines both the image of harps and the image of Christ as painter to explain how various sources of creation point to Christ and to the Father. Ephrem declares:

Who has ever played in such a marvelous and astonishing fashion,
And made a thousand cords vibrate together!
And composed with wisdom ancient things,
And also new things, with those of nature!
And since the image of the Creator is hidden in them,
On them, you have shown your outline;
And starting with them, the Lord of all ap-

31

peared to us,
And also the Son of the Lord of all.

Dispersed symbols, You have gathered
and You have exposed the prototypes of your
Announcing (Gospel)
And the prowess and signs borrowed from nature,
You have mixed such colors for your image;
You have contemplated Yourself (as in a mirror)
and You have painted Yourself,
O Painter who have painted Your Father in Yourself.
The One by the Other You have painted Yourself.[22]

In his _Hymn against Heresies_, 28, Ephrem reiterates these themes with the image of Christ as husbandman: "Look and see how nature and Scripture are yoked together for the Husbandman..."[23]

If the Christian follows the way of symbols, he will reach Christ. In fact, Ephrem in the _Hymn on Virginity, No. 10_, portrays Christ as a "Blessed Sea", and symbols are a torrent of streams that empty into Christ.[24] In more than one place, Ephrem uses the image of streams to describe how Christ summarizes all that came before him. For example, in the _Hymn on Ephiphany, No. 4_, he says:

In the Scriptures He is written of; on
Nature He is impressed; His crown is figured in
kings, in prophets His truth, His atonement in
priests.
...Lo! the prophets have poured out on
Him, their glorious mysteries; the priests and
kings have poured out upon Him, their wonderful
types: they all have poured them out on all of
Him.
Christ overcame and surpassed, by His
teachings the mysteries, by His interpretations
the parables; as the sea into its midst receives all streams.[25]

Christ is the door of all goods, the term of all mysteries, and the treasure of all parables. Before him there were only symbols and shadows, with him there is the truth. Ephrem has a dynamic view of the mysteries of the Old Testament: they await Christ, march toward him, and they flow into Him. P. Yousif sees in this approach a principle of appropriation. Persons have passed but not their work nor their mystery. Christ has taken royalty, prophecy, and priesthood. He takes something from us to give us something. What the symbols prefigure comes to reside in Christ.[26]

In his Hymn on Virginity No. 9, Ephrem expresses the view that Christ especially in his crucifixion is the consummation of all mysteries and figures:

At the coming of our Sun,
The lamps have accomplished their task and passed
And the figures and mysteries have ended;
by the invisible circumcision.
...
For it is Christ who has achieved
the mysteries (of the Scriptures) by his wood
Their figures by (in) his body
their adornments by his beauty
And they have all been consummated in him entirely![27]

Ephrem's theology of symbol can be used to explain the work of redemption. L. Leloir notes that Ephrem views the human body itself in the role of symbol. Every body which bears the sign of the first Adam is nourishment for death; but everyone who bears the sign of the second Adam is a master over death. Bodies die because they have sinned, and earth which is their mother has been cursed; but the body which is the Church is incorruptible, and the earth of which it is born is blessed, for this earth is Mary, blessed among women. Since Adam died because of sin, it was necessary that He remove sin and thereby also remove death; His eucharistic body replaces now the fruit of the tree, and the eucharistic table has become for us the garden of Eden.[28]

In his Hymn on Virginity, No. 11, Ephrem gives several examples of how various things in nature produce their result through a form of suffering or self-destruction. For Ephrem, they all symbolize the salvific suffering of Christ. He concludes by saying:

Behold all these things
teach with their symbols
that they release by their suffering
the treasure of their riches;
and that the suffering of the Son of the most

33

Good
is the key to his treasures.[29]

One final aspect of the idea of typology is that
it is progressive. The "time of the Church" is fulfillment or reality when compared to Old Testament
types, but the Church, on the other hand, is a type of
the eschatological kingdom. According to R. Murray,
Ephrem portrays history as a road on which humanity has
journeyed. In his Hymns against Heresies, the way laid
down by God stretches from the Tree (of Life) to the
Cross: from the 'wood' to the 'wood', and from Eden to
Zion, from Zion to the holy Church, and from the Church
to the Kingdom.[30]

Presumed in God's revelation through types and
symbols is the idea that humans are therefore free to
accept or reject God's revelation. God does not deal
with humans by force but respects freedom of choice.
Ephrem explains:

See his kindness!  Though he could have made us
fair
by force, without toil, he has toiled in every
way
that we might become fair by our own choice,
ourselves the artists of our own fairness
using the colors our own freedom had gathered.
(Hymn on the Faith, No. 31)[31]

As we have mentioned above, in the Syriac view
God is mysterious even in his revelation. On the one
hand, the only proper human response to God is silence;
on the other, God has manifested himself in created
forms. Ephrem states the position very clearly:

Man is too small to understand all languages:
if he could understand the language of the
watchful spirits,
then perhaps he could rise to understand the
silence
which is spoken between the Father and the Son.

Our language is foreign to the voice of animals,
the language of the Watchers to every language.
The silence in which the Father speaks to his
Son
is foreign (even) to the Watchers.

34

O his kindness! as he put on all forms for us
to see,
so he put on all voices in order to teach us.
His nature is one, it can be seen:
His silence is one, it can be heard. (Hymn on
the Faith, No. 11)[32]

Notes to Chapter Three

1. Cited by R. Murray, "The Theory of Symbolism in St. Ephrem's Theology," Parole de l'Orient (Melanges offerts au R.P. Francois Graffin, S.J.), vols. 6-7 (1975-6) pp. 11, 16.

2. A. de halleux, "Mar Ephrem Theologien," Parole de l'Orient, vol. 4 (1973) p. 45.

3. Ibid., pp. 45-6.

4. R. Murray, "A Hymn of St. Ephrem to Christ on the Incarnation, the Holy Spirit, and the Sacraments," Eastern Churches Review, vol. 3 (1970) p. 147.

5. G. Saber, "La Typlologie Sacramentaire et Baptismale de Saint Ephrem," Parole de l'Orient, vol. 4 (1973) pp. 76-9.

6. P. Yousif, "Symbolisme christologique dans la Bible et dans la nature chez S. Ephrem de Nisibe," Parole de l'Orient, vol. 8 (1977-8) p.48.

7. Murray, "The Theory of Symbolism...," p. 2.

8. S. Brock, "The Poet as Theologian," Sobornost, 7.4 (1977) pp. 244-5; S. Brock, The Harp of the Spirit, p. 6.

9. Cited by G. Saber, La Theologie Baptismale (Kaslik: Universite de Saint-Esprit, 1974), p. 36

10. Brock, Harp, p. 65.

11. Cited by Saber, art. cit., p. 83. See also: Murray, "A Hymn of St. Ephrem to Christ...," p. 147.

12. de Halleux, art. cit., p. 47.

13. Brock, Harp, p. 11. See also: Alain Desreumaux, "Une Homélie Syriaque Anonyme sur la Nativite," Parole de l'Orient, vols. 6-7 (1975-6) pp. 195-203.

14. Yousif, art. cit, p. 46.

15. Murray, "The Theory of Symbolism...," pp. 3 ff.

16. Cited by S. Brock, "World and Sacrament in the Writings of the Syriac Fathers," Sobornost, 6.10 (1974) p. 692.

17. Brock, Harp, p. 59.

18. Douglas Fox, The "Matthew-Luke Commentary" of Philoxenus (Missoula: Scholars' Press, 1979), p. 252.

19. Brock, "Poet...," p. 244.

20. T. Jansma, "Encore le Credo de Jacques de Saroug," L'Orient Syrien, vol. 10 (1965) p. 334.

21. Yousif, art. cit., pp. 62-3.

22. Ibid., p. 59.

23. Cited by Brock, Harp, p. 10.

24. Yousif, art. cit., p. 34.

25. Nicene and Post-Nicene Fathers, p. 272.

26. Yousif, art. cit., pp. 9, 55; L. Leloir, Doctrines et méthodes de S. Ephrem d'après son Commentaire de l'Evangile concordant (original syriaque et version arménienne), Corpus Scriptorum Christianorum Orientalium (Louvain, 1961), vol. 220, p. 41; El-Khoury, "Gen. 1, 26 -- Dans l'Interpretation de Saint Ephrem...," OCA, vol. 205 (1978) p. 201.

27. Yousif, art. cit., pp. 25-7.

28. Leloir, op. cit., p. 43.

29. Yousif, art. cit., p. 42.

30. Murray, "The Theory of Symbolism...," p. 8.

31. Ibid., p. 17.

32. Ibid., p. 18.

# CHAPTER FOUR

## INCARNATION

The Incarnation represents the fullness of revelation and the climax of human creation. In its redemptive aspect, it remedies the effects of sin. Sin had introduced disharmony between heaven and earth, and among humankind. Humans created in the image of God, now possessed a distorted image, and were unable to benefit from the grace of God's indwelling. Sin had also lead humans into darkness and ignorance. The Word of God, both the instrument and model of creation, now brings about its fulfillment in history. Possessed with the glory that he had from the beginning, he undergoes a second birth to reconcile heaven and earth, and to enable humans to share again in the divine nature. Christ not only heals human sinfulness, but teaches us through his light and shows us the way to the Father. The Syriac fathers view Christ's redemptive work as resulting from his entry into three wombs: the womb of Mary, the waters of the Jordan, and the depths of 'sheol'. By overcoming the kingdom of death and providing us with Baptism, Christ brings about new life and new creation. In this chapter, we will consider the Incarnation and its effects, while we will study the meaning of the Cross, death and resurrection in the next chapter.

According to Ephrem, the Word became incarnate to heal all creatures. He asked his Father to give him the glory which he possessed with the Father before the creation of the world. The glory with which he was clothed at the time creatures were created, and with which humans had also been clothed. The Word sought this glory to restore the primitive harmony of creation.[1] In his Commentary on the Gospel, 14, 17, Ephrem explains:

> Following the sin of Adam, creatures had put on corruption, according to the word of the Apostle ⟨Romans 8, 20⟩, so that the Son of the Creator came to heal them...Wishing to restore and accomplish the primitive order of creation, he asked for that glory of which he was vested at the time when creatures were vested ⟨wearing light as a garment according to Ps 104, 2⟩. For in the same way that he created by grace the primitive essence of creatures, vesting

them in glory and magnificence; so by mercy, there would be a re-formation, also immaculate, by the glory that he wears.

Ephrem uses a kind of analogy to show that just as the Incarnation was a second birth for Christ, so humans must have a second birth to be redeemed. In a Memra on Our Lord, Ephrem states:

> The First-Born according to his ⟨divine⟩ nature, was born a second time outside his nature; so that we who have a natural ⟨human⟩ birth, would know of a second birth which is available to us. For, just as the spiritual One could not have become corporeal without a bodily birth, so we cannot become spiritual without a spiritual birth.

The Maronite liturgy reflects this idea of a double birth in the "sedro" for the fourth Sunday of Easter which says: "O Uncreated Son through whom all things were created, You were begotten of the Father from all eternity and were born of the Virgin Mary in the fullness of time..."

## "Clothed in the flesh"

The most common term used by the Syriac fathers to describe the Incarnation is that Christ "put on the body" or "clothed himself in the body". Aphraat sees Jacob clothing Joseph as a type of the Father sending the Son to put on the body. According to Robert Murray, Aphraat uses the phrase frequently and sees in the action of Christ's putting on the body a source of our resurrection. However, Aphraat never develops the idea of the solidarity of Christ's body with our bodily nature.2

On the other hand, in his Hymn on the Nativity, No. 7, Ephrem speaks of Christ as a "maker" like His Father, who made for himself a body and "clothed himself" in it. In his Incarnation, he brings mercy from his Father and "clothes our weakness with glory."3 Ephrem also speaks of the "garment ⟨i.e. the body⟩ of the Lord" as a vehicle of healing. In the "visible dress" of Christ "dwells hidden power."4 Ephrem extends the image of clothing to describe the mystery of the Eucharist. In the Hymn on the Faith, No. 19, he explains:

40

Who is worthy of your garment, the dress of
your humanity?
Who is worthy of your body, the dress of your
godhead?
Two dresses are yours, O Lord,
the garment <of> the body, and the Bread, the
bread of life.
Who would not wonder at the dress of your changing?
See, the body veiled your splendor, your awesome nature.
Your clothing veiled your weaker nature;
the bread veils the Fire that dwells within it. [5]

Murray speculates that the encratism of the
Acts of Thomas might be influenced by the conviction
that Christ by 'putting on the body' sancitified it and
made continence possible. [6]

The Maronite liturgy preserves this image in the
response to the Trisagion on the feast of Nativity with
the prayer: "O Christ, who was clothed in the flesh,
have mercy on us..."

## The reconciling of heaven and earth

In the view of the Syriac fathers, the most per-
vasive effect of the Incarnation was the reconciliation
of the heavens and the earth. In his Commentary on the
Diatesseron, Ephrem explains that Christ was at the
same time both visible man and hidden God. In his
Incarnation Christ achieves the reconciliation of
heaven and earth by his flesh being drawn to his divinity. [7] For Ephrem, the act of 'kenosis' is the act of
reconciliation. In the Hymn on the Nativity, No. 3, he
declares: "...Your day reconciled heaven and earth,
because therein the Highest came down to the lowest." [8]
In his Hymn on the Unleavened Bread, Ephrem expands on
this idea and implies that it brings about human sanctification:

Your mercy, I admire
You have extended it to sinners
You impoverished your greatness
to enrich our misery
so that we become, by your goodnes in our regard
companions of the beings on high. [9]

The Maronite liturgy reflects this teaching in the <u>Anaphora of III Peter</u> which declares: "Yes, we ask You, unique Son of the Father, by whom Peace has conversed with us, Son of the Highest, in whom the high and low were reconciled..." Also, in the 'prayer of forgiveness' of the Visitation to Elizabeth Sunday, we find the following: "May we be worthy to praise, confess, and glorify the Lord of all eternity who hid Himself in the womb of a virgin; the 'Ancient of Days' who has concealed himself in the virgin's temple; the everlasting God who joined heaven and earth by communing with a simple maiden..."

## Sharing in the divine nature

As indicated above, the second birth of Christ becomes the basis of our own divinization. Through the Incarnation, humans without ceasing to be so, take on a new dimension through Baptism, as sons and daughters of God. This was the role intended for humans from the beginning of creation. They had been created to be children of God, but through the misuse of free-will had not fulfilled their intended role.[10]

Ephrem uses a variety of images to express this truth. In the <u>Homily on our Lord</u>, he speaks of the Word changing his dwelling place and thus bring about our own elevation. He states:

> ...Glory to the One who departed from one dwelling place to take up his abode in another! That He might come to make us a dwelling-place for his Sender, the Only-Begotten departed from (being) with Deity and took up His abode in the Virgin; that by a common manner of birth, though only-begotten, He might become the brother of many. And He departed from sheol and took up His abode in the Kingdom; that He might seek out a path from sheol which oppresses all, to the Kingdom which requites all.[11]

Our sanctification through sharing a common humanity with Christ is explicitly stated in the Homily on our Lord: "...Glory be to Him who received from us that He might give to us; that through that which is ours we might more abundantly receive of that which is His!"[12]

As we shall see, the sanctification of humans

42

through incorporation in the divinity of Christ is extended through the mysteries (sacraments). Jesus receives the Spirit in Baptism that we may also be born of the Spirit;[13] and the incoporation into Christ occurs especially in the Eucharist. Ultimately, this sanctification will occur in the Church.[14]

The Maronite liturgy celebrates this joining with Christ in the 'prayer of intinction': You have united, O Lord, Your divinity with our humanity; and our humanity with your divinity; Your life with our mortality and our mortaltiy with Your life. You have assumed what is ours and You have given us what is yours for the life and salvation of our souls. To you be glory forever." This same prayer is found in the Anaphora of III Peter and in the "sedro" of the Morning Office for Holy Thursday. This theme is also in the "sedro" of the Baptismal liturgy, which declares: "...By sharing our human nature, weakened through Adam's sin, you enabled us to share in your divnity, and to receive the gift of life..."

With this new creation is the dispelling of sin. In the Nisibene Hymn, No. 35, Ephrem explains: "...Sin again said, it must be, that I forsake, and change from that which I am; for this Son of Mary who is come, as a new creation, has created mankind."[15]

### Renewal of our 'image'

For Ephrem, the original image of Adam, disfigured and lost in the Fall, is found and restored by Christ as the "image of God". For the Christian, the ultimate restoration occurs in Baptism and the new life of faith.[16]

In the Homily on the Nativity, Ephrem explains: "Of His love He came down to renew the image of Adam grown old." He goes on to say that the day of Christ's birth resembles the first day of creation. Just as creation was established on the first day, it is now renewed. The earth is now blessed, where with Adam's sin it had been cursed. Where death had been introduced into the world, with Christ we have life again.[17]

Ephrem believes also that in receiving anew God's image, humans are able to turn their wills from evil. In his Hymn on the Nativity, No 1., he explains that just as the Incarnation in a sense involved the "Lord of nature going against his nature", so we should

43

not find it so difficult to convert from our evil wills. While our body is fixed in its nature, our wills have such dominion that their possiblities for growth are unlimited. God has imprinted himself on humanity, so that we might be adorned with his imprint[18]

In his Hymn on the Nativity, No. 12, Ephrem extends the action of renewal to all of creation:

...you Churches also, <desire> that the Son of the Creator who came to renew all creatures, may adorn you!
He received the foolish who worshipped and served all the stars; He renewed the earth which was worn out through Adam, who sinned and waxed old. The new formation was the creature of its Renewer, and the all-sufficient One repaired the bodies along with their wills[19]

In the Maronite liturgy, the Anaphora of James declares that when humans had gone astray, God the Father did not abandon them but called them back by the law and the prophets; "...and when the time was fulfilled You sent your Son into the world that He might renew your image." The "sedro" of the Evening Office for the Wednesdays of Lent prays: "...You have taken our image to give us yours; you have fasted from food and drink to redeem Adam who had eaten the forbidden fruit and so you have restored the image that human greediness had damaged, and have rendered to humans the assurance and joy that they had lost."

## Clothed with glory

In the Syriac mind, with the restoration of the image of God that Adam had distorted, comes the return of the 'robe of glory'. In the Hymn on the Nativity, Ephrem explains: "On this day the Lord exchanged glory for shame, in being humble; because Adam changed the truth for unrighteousness in being a rebel. The Good One had mercy on him, justified and set right them that had turned aside."[20] In the Homily on the Nativity, Ephrem portrays Adam as rejoicing at the birth of Christ, because the glory that he lost has now been recovered.[21] In the Hymn on the Nativity, No. 1, Ephrem describes Eve as looking for Christ, since he will clothe her nakedness not with leaves, but with the same glory that she and Adam had exchanged away.[22]

44

The Incarnation is also seen as a necessary action to help the needy and sinners. First of all, it is important that God be made visible. In a <u>Homily on our Lord</u>, Ephrem explains that the divine power in itself could not be handled, and therefore had to put on a body that could be touched. Humans can draw near to him and by way of his humanity can discern his divnity.[23] Ephrem sees in Christ's putting on a created body the way to capture humans and draw them closer to God. In the <u>Hymn on the Nativity</u>, No. 14, he says:

> God saw that mankind worhsips things created: He put on a created body, that in our custom He might capture us. Lo in this our form, He that formed us healed us; and in this created shape, our Creator gave us life. He drew us not by force: blessed be he who came in ours, and joined us in His![24]

The same theme is repeated in the <u>Hymn on the Nativity</u>, No. 15.[25]

Ephrem believes that Christ's miracles of healing were also occasions for teaching. In the <u>Hymn on the Unleavened Bread</u> he explains:

> He is perfect in his goodness
> for he has combined his liberalities and his teaching
> the possessed he has cured
> in curing them, he has taught them.
> They have received to be taught.
> By the fact of being healed, they were taught.[26]

The theme of the teaching role of the incarnate Christ is reflected in the Maronite liturgy. The "sedro" of the Morning Office of the Fourth Sunday of Lent prays: "...You have sent your only Son so that the world know you and love you as you have loved Him. Christ our God, to you thanksgiving, you who made yourself like us to teach us the way which leads to the Father..." In the "sedro" of the Evening Office for Wednesday, Christ is described in this way: "...You have come, walked on earth and have traced for us a way which leads to the heavens."

## The Baptism of Christ

As indicated above, the progress of the Incarnation is seen to involve three wombs or 'staging points': Mary's womb, the womb of the Jordan, and the womb of sheol. James of Serug explains:

> He completed his whole course by three staging points: he resided in the virgin and came to birth, though he was God; he received baptism, yet he was God; and he descended to sheol, and the world recognized that he was God.

For James, Christian baptism has its origin in two different moments of the Incarnation -- Christ's baptism in the Jordan and the piercing of his side on the cross. The salvific and sacramental effects of these events will be discussed in the chapter on Christian initiation.

Since John is "the son of Levites", Christ's baptism at his hands provides the means by which the Jewish priesthood is transmitted to Christianity. This teaching is found in early Syriac tradition.[27]

## Doctrine on Christ

Ephrem and the Syriac fathers affirm the Nicene teaching of the equality of the Word with the Father, and adopt a descending Christology. The Nicene belief is clear in the prayer cited in Ephrem's Letter to Publius:

> Look at...the ray of his light,...at him who is equal in essence with his begetter, at him whose nature is commensurate with that from which he sprang, at him who is near to him, yet far from him, at him who is mingled with him, yet distant from him, who is with him and is not distant, at his right hand and not far off...[28]

In the Syriac mind, the divinity of Christ was always operating. While accepting his true humanity, it affirms the paradox that in every moment of the human life of Christ, the Divinity of Christ was controlling the world. Ephrem in the Hymn on the Nativity, No. 3 presents this belief with poetic paradox:

> ...He was silent as a Babe, and yet He was making his creatures execute all his commands. For without the First-Born no man can approach

unto the Essence, to which He is equal. The
thirty years He was in the earth, Who was or-
dering all creatures, Who was receiving all the
offerings of praise from those above and those
below. He was wholly in the depths and wholly
in the highest! He was wholly with all things
and wholly with each. While his body was for-
ming within the womb, his power was fashioning
all members! While the conception of the Son
was fashioning in the womb, He himself was
fashiong babes in the womb....For see how, when
He was wholly hanging upon the Cross, His Power
was yet making all creatures move! For He dar-
kened the sun and made the earth quake; He
rent the graves and brought forth the dead!
See who when He was wholly on the Cross, yet
again He was wholly everywhere! While on the
Cross He quickened the dead, so while a Babe He
was fasioning babes....It was by Power from Him
that Mary was able to bear in her bosom Him
that bears up all things!
...He gave imposition of hands to Moses on the
Mount, and received it in the midst of the
river from John.[29]

On the other hand, in Ephrem's view, Christ was
the perfect human. In his Commentary on the Diatesseron, he describes Christ as free from all sin and
concupiscence. He had no failings and could not be
decieved. Since Christ came as a doctor, he could not
be morally ill; and since he is the shepherd, he could
not go astray; nor as teacher, could he err; and being
the light, he could not stumble. Therefore, Christ was
perfect from his conception to his resurrection.

However, after all of our theologizing, we are
reminded that we are dealing with mystery. In the
Incarnation, we still encounter the hiddenness of God.
In the Hymn on Nativity, No. 8, Ephrem declares:

If a man should seek after your nature,
it is hidden in heaven in the mighty bosom of
the Godhead; and if a man seek after your
visible body, it is laid down before their eyes
in the lowly bosom of Mary.
The mind wanders between your generations, O Rich One! Thick folds are upon
your Godhead. Who can sound your depths, the
great Sea that made itself little?
We come to see You as God, and, lo! You

are a man: we come to see You as man, and there
shines forth the Light of your Godhead![30]

Ephrem did not deal with the Incarnation in
Greek philosophical terms. As we have seen, he expresses its truth in the richness of imagery. The term
that he was mostly likely to use regarding the two natures of Christ was 'mingle' ("mzag" in Syriac), which
he uses of Christ, and also to express the union of
humans with Him by grace and the sacraments.[31]

## "Schema"

James of Serug deals with the Incarnation by
using the term "schema". For him, it represents a
'manner or mode of existence'. For example, the schema
of a monk might be to live in the city, or in a monastery, or as a solitary. Therefore, Jesus is God by
nature, but in the image and schema of a human. He
came to dwell in the womb of the virgin in the schema
of a man, so that Mary became a "sealed letter full of
secrets". James says:

> He took the image of the servant from the womb
> of the blessed one
> And in the schema of servants he visited the
> servants and freed them.
> He dwelt in the daughter of a man, and became
> the son of man by these things...[32]

The idea of schema is a possible model for explaining the doctrine of the Incarnation. For James, a
thought (word) can exist in two schemata at the same
time: in one schema, in the mind of the writer of a
letter, and in a second, in the form of writing on a
page. In the first schema, the word is intangible and
unlimited; in the second, it is both tangible and
limited. No one has access to the thought in the mind
of another person, so long as it is in his mind; on the
other hand, one has immediate access to the same
thought if it is written down.[33]

In a further theological development, some Syriac writers see all of humanity being divinized in the
Incarnation and union of the Divine. For example,
Roberta Chesnut observes that James of Serug conceived
of human nature as a concrete collective. The Word was
united not only to the individual humanity of Jesus,
but rather, through Jesus, the Word was joined to the
whole human race. She claims that James does not make

a clear distinction between the 'mixture' of the Word in humanity in general and the 'mixture' of divinity and humanity in Jesus. By the Word being joined to humanity, the Father is brought into close relationship with the human race, and in this regard the term 'mixture' is again used. Chesnut refers to <u>Letter 19</u> of James which says that Christ came "for his Father that he should be a Father for us...and he mixed us with respect to genus with his begetter."[34]

We can conclude this chapter with a poetic summary by Ephrem on the meaning and effect of the Incarnation in the <u>Hymn on the Nativity, No. 2</u>:

> ...Glory to Him, who came to us by His firstborn! Glory to the Silence, that spoke by His Voice. Glory to the One on high, who was seen by his Day-spring! Glory to the Spiritual, who was pleased to have a Body, that in it his virtue might be felt, and He might by that Body show mercy on his household's bodies!
> ...Glory to the Hidden One, who even with the mind cannot be felt at all by them that pry into Him; but by his graciousness was felt by the hand of man!
> ...Blessed He who sealed our soul, and adorned it and espoused it to Himself. Blessed He who made our body a tabernacle for his unseen Nature. Blessed He who by our tongue interpreted his secret things.
> ...Glory to Him who loosed us, and was bound for us all! Glory to Him who gave the pledge, and redeemed it too! Glory to the Beautiful, who conformed us to his image!
> Glory to Him who sowed his light in the darkness, and was reproached in his hidden state, and covered his secret things. He also stripped and took off from us the clothing of our filthiness. Glory be to Him on high, who mixed his salt in our minds, his leaven in our souls. His Body became Bread, to quicken our deadness. [35]

## Notes to Chapter Four

1. L. Leloir, _Doctrines et Méthodes de S. Ephrem d'après son Commentaire de l'Evangile Concordant_, pp. 38-39.

2. R. Murray, _Symbols of Church and Kingdom_, pp. 69-70; 310.

3. _Nicene and Post-Nicene Fathers_, p. 240.

4. Robert Murray, "A Hymn of St. Ephrem to Christ on the Incarnation...," p. 143.

5. _Ibid._, pp. 146-7.

6. Murray, _Symbols_, p. 311.

7. Leloir, _op. cit._, p. 24.

8. _Nicene and Post-Nicene Fathers_, p. 229.

9. J. Gribomont, "Les Hymnes de Saint Ephrem sur la Pâque," _Melto_, vol. 13 (1967) pp. 154-5.

10. Sebastian Brock, "Mary and the Eucharist," _Sobornost_, 1.2 (1979) p. 52.

11. _Nicene and Post-Nicene Fathers_, p. 305.

12. _Ibid._, p. 309.

13. F.C. Burkitt, _Early Eastern Christianity_, pp. 103-4.

14. Murray, _Symbols_, p. 70.

15. _Nicene and Post-Nicene Fathers_, p. 194.

16. Kronholm, _Motifs_, p. 66.

17. Brock, _Harp_, pp. 66-8.

18. _Nicene and Post-Nicene Fathers_, p. 226.

19. _Ibid._, p. 247.

20. Nicene and Post-Nicene Fathers, p. 234.

21. Brock, Harp, p. 68.

22. Nicene and Post-Nicene Fathers, p. 224.

23. Ibid., p. 326.

24. Ibid., p. 251.

25. Ibid., p. 253.

26. Gribomont, art. cit., pp. 154-5.

27. Brock, "Baptismal themes in the Writings of James of Sarugh," pp. 325-6.

28. Brock, "Ephrem's Letter to Publius," p. 278.

29. Nicene and Post-Nicene Fathers, pp. 233-4.

30. Ibid., p. 242.

31. R. Murray, "A Hymn of St. Ephrem to Christ...," p. 147.

32. Cited by R. Chesnut, Three Monophysite Christologies, pp. 115; 122-3.

33. Ibid., pp. 123-4.

34. Ibid., p. 135.

35. Nicene and Post-Nicene Fathers, p. 227.

# CHAPTER FIVE

## REDEMPTION

The Syriac fathers do not separate the Redemption from the Incarnation of Christ in their theology. The Word of God from the beginning of time desired in his 'tenderness' to restore His image in humans who had distorted it through sin. As we have noted, in a continuous movement, the Word humbles himself and becomes flesh, enters the womb of Mary, the waters of the Jordan, and the mouth of sheol (i.e. the region of the dead) where he overcomes death and leads all humans on a path that takes them to the kingdom of the Father. The two events most focused on are the death on the cross and the descent into sheol. The cross becomes the victorious cross and the new 'tree of life'. The mysteries of Baptism, Eucharist, Crowning (i.e. marriage) and the Church are all seen as flowing from the event of the cross. The "desent into sheol" provides the imagery for the ultimate conquering of death and the prince of the underworld. Ephrem sees the whole life of Christ as redemptive. The death of Christ is the culmination of the "descent" of the son in our world, living in humilty by which he hid his mystery. Salvation results from the ascent to the right hand of the Father, triumphant over sin.[1] It is through the interweaving of various themes and imagery that the Syriac Fathers developed their teaching on redemption.

J. Gribomont claims that Ephrem ignores the Pauline doctrine of redmption and focuses on Old Testament typology. The themes of creation and paradise, and the paschal lamb are prominent. On the other hand, the mystery itself of salvation is the person of Christ. The most beautiful verses in Ephrem on redemption are those which contemplate hidden divinity on the cross, in contrast with the darkness of Golgotha.[2]

### Death on the Cross

The Cross reconciles heaven and earth

Ephrem relates the announcement of the angels at the birth of Christ with the work achieved through the cross. In his <u>Commentary on the Diatesseron,</u> he explains:

53

When he descended on the earth and put on humanity, the angels exclaimed: "Peace on earth". And when humanity mounted and was raised, plunged in divinity and seated at its right, children exclaimed before it: "Peace in the heavens, blessing in the heights". It is thus the Apostle was taught to say: by the blood of his cross, he has purified all that is in the heavens and on the earth.3

In his Hymn on the Epiphany, No. 2, Ephrem speaks of the dead receiving life through the death of Christ and clearly states the reconciliation of the heavens and the earth. He says:

In the year that is the thirtieth let them give thanks with us, the dead that have lived through His dying, the living that were converted in His Crucifixion, and the height and the depth that have been reconciled in Him!4

Ephrem extends the redemptive work to the ascension, when, in the Hymni Dispersi, No. 22, he praises Christ who by his humility saves us and gave us peace through his cross, and "elevated us by his Ascension".5

While James of Serug focuses more on the descent of Christ into sheol, his view is that as a result of the cross the human race is now in a new condition. The great wall of enmity separating the upper and lower beings from each other has been broken down; God and humans are no longer angry with each other. In fact, James uses the term "to mix" to describe the way in which the Word Incarnate brought about a reconciliation between the two "sides" who were angry with each other, God and humanity, bringing them into a state of peace. Roberta Chesnut cites James of Serug as saying:

The love of God was revealed to the world in the cross of his son, and that cross broke down the wall of enmity which the Seprent built between Adam and God, and he released the decree of that death which was given to Adam for the transgression of the commandment. And he made peace between upper beings and lower ones and he mixed the sides in each other that the first enmity should be forgotten.6

The Syriac Anaphora of St. Celestine reflects

the reconciling work of the cross in its prayer of peace: "O God, Immeasurable Sea of Tranquility and ever-flowing spring of love, by the cross of your only-begotten Son, You have removed all obstacles to harmony. You have bestowed peace and united heavenly and earthly creatures. By the power of Your Lordship, You have reconciled the world..." And the Maronite Evening Office for the Exaltation of the Cross declares: "Blessed be the cross, it is by it that peace reigns between the heights and the depths, may the light spread on the earth..."

## The Cross as bridge

If the cross is reconciler, it is natural that it should serve as a bridge between death and life. This viewpoint is also influenced by belief that the cross as 'tree' overcomes the sin that came through the tree in paradise. Ephrem explains in his <u>Homily on the Lord</u>:

This is the son of the carpenter, who skilfully made his cross a bridge over sheol that swallows up all, and brought over mankind into the dwelling of life. And because it was through the tree that mankind had fallen into sheol, so upon the tree they passed over into the dwelling of life.[7]

The Syriac fathers also draw a contrast between the sword the angel carried to keep humans out of paradise and the lance which pierced the side of Christ. Ephrem explains in his <u>Hymn on the Cross</u>:

Blessed are you, O living Wood <of the Cross>,
For you have become a lance hidden for death;
In effect, the Son struck by the lance,
has killed death at the moment where the lance pierced Him.
His lance has abolished the lance,
For his pardon has torn up the written act <of our condemnation>,
Behold Paradise of the blessed where those who ought to come out have entered
And where the rejected <have recovered> their home.[8]

In the Morning Office for Sunday, the "sedro" prays: "...admirable marvel: day before yesterday, the king was crucified and underwent suffering; today he is victorious in his Resurrection. Two days ago, the lance opened his side; today, by his goodness Baptism has been inaugurated..."

## The Church as Bride at the Cross

The redemption achieved on the Cross is also the source of the establishment of the Church. For the Syriac fathers, the Church is the bride of Christ in the Jordan, but wedded to him on the cross where her dowry is written in the blood which flowed from the side of Christ. The blood and water are also seen as symbols of Baptism and the Eucharist which make humans children of the Father and part of the saved assembly. James of Serug states:

> The Bridegroom's side has been pierced, and from it the Bride has come forth,
> fulfilling the type provided by Adam and Eve
> For from the beginning God knew and depicted
> Adam and Eve in the likeness of the image of his only-begotten;
> He slept on the cross as Adam had slept his deep sleep,
> his side was pierced and from it there came forth the Daughter of light,
> -- water and blood as image of divine children to be heirs to the Father who love his Only-begotten.
> ...
> The stillness of the sleep of death fell upon him on the cross
> and from him came forth the Mother who gives birth to all spiritual beings.
> ...
> The King's Son made a marriage feast, in blood on Golgotha;
> there the Daughter of Day was bethrothed to him, to be his,
> and the royal ring was beaten out in the nails of his hands;
> with his holy blood was the betrothal made.
> He took her hand there, seeing that she had shown her love for him at the hour of his shame;
> he set her at his right hand, to be with him.
> He led her into the Garden -- the bridal chamber he had prepared for her.[9]

The Maronite liturgy embodies this theme. In

56

the 'prayer of forgiveness' of Cana Sunday it prays:
"May we be worthy to praise, confess, and glorify the
Bridegroom who bethrothed the Church with his blood and
sacrificed himself for her..." And, the 'prayer of
forgiveness' of the wedding liturgy prays to "Jesus
Christ, the heavenly bridegroom, who, in the self-
giving of His death on the cross, established an everlasting love and fidelity toward His Bride, the
Church..."

Reflecting on the symbolism of the wood as ultimately a figure of the cross, Ephrem with complex
imagery sees the ark of Noah as sybmol of the cross, of
the Church, and of Baptism. In his Hymn on the Faith,
No. 49, he describes how the ark symbolized the cross
and the "rudder of its pilot" who came to construct the
Church "on the waters". Christ saves in the name of
the Trinity, and the Spirit in place of the "dove"
gives his salvific anointing.[10]

James of Serug offers a profound insight into
the theology of marriage by seeing in every marriage of
man and woman, a reflection of the mystery of the wedding of Church to Christ. However, this mystery was
not unveiled until the crucifixion and the subsequent
teaching of St. Paul. James of Serug in a Homily on
Moses' Veil explains:

The hidden Father betrothed a bride to his
only-begotten,
having instructed her through prophecy in a
symbolic way.
In his love he built a great palace for the
bride of light
and depicted the bridegroom in various ways in
her royal home.
Moses entered in and, like a skilled artist,
delineated
the bridegroom and the bride, and then covered
the great picture with a veil.
He put in his writings that 'a man should leave
his father and mother
and cleave to his wife, so that the two of
them might be one completely.'
...
he covered up his words by various means,
hiding them from outsiders.
And so he painted a picture inside the chamber
of the royal bridegroom;
he called them 'man and woman', although he

knew the truth,
that the one was Christ and the other the
Church, both being veiled...
    After the wedding feast <i.e. the redemptive
mysteries> Paul entered in and beheld
the veil lying there; he seized and removed it
from the fair couple
    ...and began to show what the covered picture
was:
'in those called "man and wife" in the prophetic writings
I recognize Christ and his Church, the two
being one.'
    ...
    The bethrothed made the daughter of day to
enter a new womb,
and the testing waters of baptism were in la-
bour and gave rebirth to her:
he rested in the water and invited her: she
went down, clothed herself in him and ascended...[11]

## Baptism and the Eucharist

        As noted above, the cross is seen as the
source of Baptism. For James of Serug: "Christ came
and opened up baptism on his cross...water and blood,
for the fashioning of spiritual children flowed, and
Baptism became the mother of the living."[12]

        Philoxenus of Mabboug repeats this theme when he
says: "'There came forth blood and water': baptismal
water together with the blood that brings absolution;
by water the font was indicated, by blood the Holy Mysteries which cleanse us from sin every time we receive
them."[13]

        The Maronite liturgy restates this teaching in
the 'epiklesis' over the baptismal water when it declares: "...Let it <the water> become as the water that
flowed from the side of your only Son upon the cross,
so that it may purify and cleanse all who are baptized
in it..."

## The Cross as 'tree of life'

        With their feel for imagery, the Syriac fathers
saw an intimate connection between the cross of calvary
and the tree of the garden of Eden and ultimately the
'tree of life'. In fact, according to legend the cross

was the descendent of the tree of life by its seeds.[14]
Ephrem in his Hymn on Virginity declares:

> He has come among us in his love, he, the
> blessed tree!
> The wood <of the cross> has abolished the wood,
> the fruit has been suppressed by the fruit
> and the tormentor by the Living One![15]

Ephrem points to the connection more bluntly in his
Nisibene Hymn, No. 58:

> ...the bosom and wings of the Cross, He opened
> in his mercy: its pinions bowed and bore the
> nations, to go to Eden. It is akin to the Tree
> of Life, and unto the son of its stock: it
> leads its beloved that on its boughs, they may
> feed on its fruits.[16]

In the Armenian Hymn, No. 49, Ephrem contrasts
the Old Testament reference to water coming forth from
the rock to nourish the Jews, to the cross as a font of
life and nourishment for the Gentiles, who are now the
'Church of the Nations'. He explains that just as the
water from the rock strengthened the Jewish people, so
the cross is a fountain of life for the Gentiles.
While the sword had guarded the tree of life, now the
"Lord of the Tree" has given himself as food for the
Gentiles. As Adam had food from the trees of paradise,
so the "Planter of Eden" has become food for us. While
we went forth from paradise with Adam, now that the
Christ has removed the lance, we are able to re-
enter.[17]

Robert Murray is of the opinion that the use of
oil or chrism in Christian initiation, and other rites
of anointing might be connected to the idea that consecrated oil comes from the tree of life, which also
at times ia used as a symbol of Christ.[18]

The Maronite liturgy speaks about the cross as
the tree of life in the "sedro" of the Evening Office
for the Exaltation of the Cross. It prays: "...In
paradise the tree of life symbolized your cross, and
Moses showed a sign of it when he extended his arms to
save the people....it is the wood of the cross of which
the wood of the ark of Noah, vessel of salvation, was
the image...

Whether it be that the cross was seen as a symbol of the work of redemption or that it possessed mystical qualities as the tree of life, or the tradition that the act of being 'signed' affords protection, there are a number of references in the Maronite liturgy to the Cross as a defence against evil. In the same "sedro" cited above, the prayer continues: "...Be for us night and day the attentive guardian which does not permit evil to overcome us..." The Office goes on in the chant before the Scripture readings to pray: "...May your cross be a protective rampart for the Church your spouse and may evil not overcome her children..." In the dismissal prayer of the Anaphora of St. Peter, we find: "O Lord, bless all the faithful who humble themselves before You and imprint on them the victorious sign of your cross that they may be protected from every evil, known and unknown..."

Nevertheless in speaking of the death of Christ on the Cross, Ephrem and the Syriac writers are aware continually of his abiding divinity. Ephrem in his Hymn on the Unleavend Bread expresses the paradox:

It is by the power which comes from him <Jesus>
that the wood bore him;
and the wood has not burnt
even though it carried fire! [19]

We may conclude this section on the significance of the Cross for the theology of redemption by again citing from Ephrem's writings, which as indicated above, describe the going out and ultimate return of Christ. Ephrem explains:

The Merciful one has looked down and has seen the soul in the abyss
and has opened a way for it to extricate itself
Even if a <simple> sign on his part would suffice.
He has imprinted his love on his work,
in putting on humanity;
<then> he appropriated <human> ignorance
to lead humans to his knowledge.
He has chanted to humans on his harp his humble chants
so that humans be raised to the heights;
He has raised his cross toward the heights
so that the children <of Eve> climb toward the heavenly <beings>. [20]

## The Descent into Sheol

It is the descent into sheol that completes the work of redemption. The kingdom of death must be defeated and deceased humans, especially Adam must be liberated and recovered. James of Serug influenced by Philippians 2, 16 usually speaks of the Son of God who has the appearance of a servant and is not recognized by the demons because of his humility and suffering. Christ's true identity is revealed in the crucifixion. By his descent into sheol, he triumphs over the empire of death and gloriously returns to the Father in the company of liberated prisoners.[21]

James of Serug has Christ seeking the lost Adam even on the occasion of his Baptism. He presents Christ as saying to John the Baptiser: "I am trying to find the lost Adam; let me go down and look for Adam..." In fact, Christ's baptism and the descent into sheol are often considered together.[22]

The descent into sheol is the principal image used by the Syriac fathers to describe the cosmic struggle between Christ, who ultimately is the creator of life, and the power of death and sin. Jesus by the instrumentality of the Cross had to overcome the 'dragon-serpent'. Humanity left to itself, in which sin reigned, was incapable of overcoming the dragon. It is Christ, the victorious king and son of David, who by his glorious cross has reduced the powerful evil one to silence.[23]

For the Syriac fathers, the action of Christ's descent into sheol becomes a guarantee of life and resurrection for all humans. Ephrem observes that only Christ could go to a place from where no one could come out, and then come forth without any power being able to hinder him.[24]

In the Nisibene Hymns, No. 37, Ephrem explains that only the creator could be in reality the redeemer. He says:

...No other strange key into the gate of sheol could ever be fitted.
One is the key of the Creator, that which has opened it, yes, it is to open at his coming.
Who is he that is able to join the bones, save that Power which created them/

61

What is it that shall reunite the shreds of the
body, save the hand of the Maker?
What is it that shall restore the forms, save
the finger of the Creator? He, who created and
turned and destroyed, is He that is able also
to renew and raise up. Another God is unable
to enter in and restore creatures not his own.[25]

Ephrem also explains that Christ's work was a
free act of his will which overcame death against
death's will. He also points out that it was necessary
for Christ to have a body if this confrontation with
death was to occur. In a Homily on our Lord, he says:

...This is He who made Himself subject to and
endured death of His own will, that He might
cast down death against his will. For our Lord
bore His cross and went forth according to the
will of death: but He cried upon the cross and
brought forth the dead from within sheol
against the will of Death.
...And because Death was not able to devour
Him without the body, nor sheol to swallow Him
up without the flesh, He came unto the Virgin,
that from thence He might obtain that which
should bear him to sheol...[26]

There are various images used to describe how
death was defeated. Ephrem makes the declaration that
Jesus is victorious because He is indeed the 'Living
One'. He says in the Hymn on the Nativity, No. 3: "The
Living One by His death emptied Hell <sheol>; He un-
loosed it and let fly away from it entire multitudes![27]
More concretely, Ephrem in Nisibene Hymn, No. 36 refers
to Christ as the "medicine of life". He presents death
as saying: "...the medicine of life has entered sheol
and brought its dead back to life. Who is it who has
introduced for me and hidden the living fire in which
the cold and dark wombs of sheol melt?"[28]

From the idea that Jesus is the medicine of
life, there developed the theory that while death is
portrayed as the devourer of humans, he not only could
not swallow Christ, but rather 'disgorged' Christ and
all other human beings with him. In the Homily on the
Lord, Ephrem explains that Mary conceived new life from
the ancient vine of Eve, and when death came to feed on
"mortal fruits", he swallowd the "life that is the
slayer of death". Having swallowed the medicine of

life, death was sickened and vomited forth all the living ones that he had previously swallowed.[29] James of Serug adopts the same imagery, but claims that Christ acted as a poison within death, and that Death choked on him and died.[30]

In the Hymn on the Epiphany, No. 2, Ephrem presents Christ in an active role: "...let <us> give thanks to the Son, for He it was Who on his feet entered Sheol and spoiled it and came forth; blessed be His Resurrection."[31] More specific are the references to Christ as the Light who removes darkness from sheol. In Nisibene Hymn, No. 41, Ephrem declares: "...Death opened the gates of sheol and there shone from it the splendor of the face of our Lord..."[32]

Ephrem even uses the imagery of Christ as wheat sown in sheol itself. He describes Christ as a seed of wheat who falls to sheol, but springs up as a "whole sheaf, as the new Bread".[33]

Narsai reflects a similar theology and imagery of redemption. He portrays Christ as an athelete who goes into conflict and is victorious. For Narsai, Adam was led into error by the "Deciever". Christ consented to die so that humans would not be the slaves of the Evil one. As an athelete, Christ battled with Satan and conquered him. On the cross he "fought the slayer of men, and made him a laughing-stock before angels and men".[34]

The Maronite liturgy has many references to the victory over sheol. In the Evening Office for the feast of the Resurrection, the "qolo" prays: "...to the glory of the Father, governor of all creatures, who has sent His only Son to renew his corrupted image. By his will he has opened the tomb, he has overwhelmed death and destroyed sheol. He reigns on earth and in heaven." The "sougito" of the Office adds: "...Hell <sheol> full of dead has become a desert, while the interior of the garden of Eden is filled with a crowd. Our savior has risen and he has raised with him all the saints who were asleep....We render thanks to his mercies, because by his resurrection, he has liberated Adam from his slavery." Finally, the "Bo'uto dmar Ya'qub" of the same Office uses legendary imagery when it says: "...The Powerful One of the ages roared in Sheol and its foundations tottered. And death lamented and lost his crown, becoming a mockery." [35]

The Maronite Office for Easter also declares the following about Christ in its "sedro":

...You performed marvels during your stay among the dead; you have liberated prisoners by your resurrection; you have dispersed the darkness from the creatures on whom perdition had reigned; by your voice of life you have awakened the souls of just and righteous humans, who had reposed in the sleep of death. Reducing to nothing the power of the merciless enemy, you have made calm and peace to reign in hell <sheol>, and you have gathered the people so that they adore you and announce your salvation in the entire world...

The descent into sheol has as its ultimate purpose the liberating of Adam. In the mind of the Syriac writers, Adam was the original image of God and the representative of all humans. Ephrem dwells on this theme often in his Nisibene Hymns. In Hymn No. 65 he speaks of Christ descending and plunging after Adam to deliver him from sheol and restore him to Eden.[36] The redemption of Adam is linked to the 'Mysteries' that came forth from the side of Christ. In Nisibene Hymn, No. 39, Ephrem explains: "...there came out from Him water and blood; Adam washed and lived, and returned to Paradise."[37]

In the liberating of Adam, all humans are saved. In his Nisibene Hymn, No. 36, Ephrem portrays death as speaking to Christ as king and asking him to take Adam as 'booty'. Since all the dead were hidden in Adam, they have been vivified by Christ in his coming to sheol. Not only does death surrender Adam, but since Christ now reigns over all, death in submission will have all the dead rise to meet Christ at the sound of the trumpet.[38]

Roberta Chesnut points out that James of Serug sees the necessity of Christ's going to sheol not just to liberate Adam, but to save 'the Great Adam' or 'the Great Image', the Image of the Father. For James, "the image of God was perishing in sheol, and the Son descended to seek and find the image of his Father which was perishing." Therefore, the title of Christ as 'the second Adam' has great signficance for James.[39]

In the Maronite liturgy, the "mazmoro" verse for the Sunday after Epiphany declares: "Glory to You, O

64

Abundant Giver, who rose incorruptible from the tomb. You raised the body of Adam and returned to Him who sent you." The Evening Office of Resurrection in its "qolo" chants about Christ: "...he has given joy by his resurrection to Adam who lay in sheol, has liberated him with all his children and led them to paradise full of happiness." [40]

## Other Effects of the Redemption

### Light and Truth

Light, as we have noted, is a primordial symbol of God, and has been used biblically to manifest the themes of truth and goodness. Sin is characterized by darkness, ignorance, and confusion. Therefore, one of the direct effects of Christ's redemptive work is the reappearance of light. In his Homily on the Nativity, Ephrem declares first regarding Mary: "...from her the luminous One has shone forth and dispelled the darkness of paganism." He continues: "Therefore, this day resembles the first day of creation..." [41]

T. Kronholm observes that Ephrem fought against the Bardaisanite and Manichean conception of darkness as a self-dependent entity. Therefore, Ephrem sees a close connection between the creation of light in the beginning as a victory over darkness, and Christ's victory over the darkness spread over the world by Satan. [42]

Related to the theme of light are the ideas of truth and knwoledge. Ephrem declares that knowledge of Christ drives away error from humanity which had become lost. Christ, on the other hand, leads astray and confounds the Evil One. [43] In the Hymn on the Nativity, No. 15, Ephrem explains:

Sin had spread its wings, and covered all things, that none could discern, of himself or from above, the truth. Truth came down into the womb, came forth and rolled away error.

. . .

Sin had spread out her nets for the draught. Praise be to Your birth that captured the nets of delusion. The soul took flight on high, which had been taken in the deep. [44]

In the Maronite liturgy, the Morning Office for Good Friday proclaims: "Eternal incomprehensible Light

who has been clouded voluntarily on the Cross so that
the light of his kingdom would illumine all creatures
from the beacon of the cross; Lord, illumine us and
give us joy by the sight of the glorious light and by
the manifestation of your astonishing appearance..."[45]
The hymn of light for the Morning Office prays: "The
light of the just and the joy of righteous hearts is
Christ Jesus Our Lord who has manifested himself to us
from the bosom of the Father. He has come to deliver
us from darkness and he has illumined us by his admirable light...His glory shines on the world and
brightens the depths of the abyss. He annihilates
death, puts darkness to flight, having broken the gates
of sheol. Creatures placed in darkness from former
times have adorned themselves with light; the dead who
lay in the earth have stood erect again, they chant for
they have a Savior."

Related to the theme of truth and knowledge is
the idea of remembrance. Ephrem in his Hymns on Virginity speaks about the "...Remembrance which routed
forgetfulness from creation!" Christ is God's remembrance of his suffering children, but also the restoration of man's power to remember God effectively and
enter into life-giving relationship with him."[46]

Freedom from exile and bondage

A prominent biblical image of redemption is
freedom from exile or bondage. Ephrem in his Hymn on
the Nativity, No. 19 describes freedom as becoming en-
slaved, and that Christ came as a slave to liberate
freedom. He even suffered being stricken on the face
by servants, so that "he broke the yoke that was on the
free".[47]

The prayer after the Preface in the Anaphora of
the Twelve Apostles tells us that Christ "delivered us
from exile, and saved us by his divine plan." The
Night Prayer of the Maronite Office says: "O Sunday,
you are the day when the Holy Church which was sad has
rejoiced; when the Son of the King has liberated her
from captivity and signed her with his blood..."

In his Hymns on Virginity, Ephrem sees the redemption of Christ as applying directly to the Gentiles. He says that "Grace has become a hyssop and
purified the Gentiles in his mercy." Christ is the
rock on which the "building of the Gentiles" was established. He is the "grape" that produced the medicine

of life. Robert Murray explains that the reference to the 'rock' refers to the rock spoken of in the parable at the end of the 'sermon on the mount'.[48]

A frequent image used by Syriac writers is the biblical image of Christ as the redeeming shepherd. Ephrem describes Christ flying down in search of Adam, the sheep that had strayed. He finds him and carries him back.[49] In the Nisibene Hymn, No. 52, Ephrem describes Christ as the Son of the Shepherd of all "who delivers His flock from the secret wolves that devoured it, the Evil One and Death!"[50]

In the liturgy, the Syriac Anaphora of Peter III prays to: "...the Good Shepherd who <have> given up your life for your flock and <have> delivered it from destroying wolves. Merciful Lord who from the cross hurled a cry and regathered us from being led astray..." The Maronite Morning Office for Easter Wednesday develops the theme further. In the "sedro" it prays: "O Christ, you have entered the sheepfold by the door, that is, by your incarnation, so you entered into your resurrerction by the door that was your cross, and into life by the door that was your death, for you are the door, the resurrection and the life. Those who enter by you are saved; they shall enter and rise with the liberty of children and shall find in you abundant pasture..."

Meditating on the Scriptures, the Syriac writers see Christ not only as the shepherd but also as the Passover lamb. For Ephrem Christ as Lamb brings about a double exodus -- of the Gentiles from error, and of the dead from sheol. In the Hymn on the Unleavened Bread, No. 3, he explains that with the "true lamb" there took place an exodus from error. With the "living lamb", there was a further exodus of the dead from sheol, as from Egypt. With the original passover lamb, Egypt was forced to surrender against its custom, so with the living lamb, sheol had to give back the dead against its nature. With the "cry which he uttered" the true lamb "has trodden out a path from the grave for those who lie buried".[51]

Ephrem also explains that a sinless offering was needed by a sinless priest. He extends this thinking to the sacrificial aspect of the Eucharist. In the Hymn on the Unleavend Bread, he declares:

For the spotted priests

were not worthy to offer
the Immaculate Lamb.
He made himself the peaceful offering
and purified high and low
by his blood which is all peace.

With his hands He broke the bread
symbol of the sacrifice of his body,
with his hands He mixed the Cup
symbol of the sacrifice of his blood.
He offered himself in sacrifice,
priest of our reconciliation.[52]

Ephrem develops a similar theme in his _Hymns on Virginity_. He describes Christ as the "acceptable offering", "a sacrifice self-offered with power to make us holy". Christ supersedes the blood of the animals of the old covenant. He is the lamb who is also the priest.[53]

Ephrem on more than one occasion summarizes the work of redemption. In his _Letter to Publius_, he refers to Christ as:

"...the gate of salvation, the way of truth, the propitiary lamb, the purificatory sacrifice, the priest who removes guilt, the purifying sprinkling....the renewer of nature, who gives life to mortality, who dispels the cloud of darkness, who brings to nought the power of iniquity, who weakens the hand of sheol, who breaks the sin of wickedness, who brings out the captives into the light, who raises up those prostrate in perdition, the dispeller of darkness, the establisher of rest, who opens the mouths that are closed, who gives breath to the soul as of old." [54]

## Notes to Chapter Five

1. J. Gribomont, "Le triomphe de Pacques d'après S. Ephrem," Parole de l'Orient, vol. 4 (1973) pp. 148, 158-9, 185.

2. J. Gribomont, "Les Hymnes de Saint Ephrem sur la Pâque," Melto, vol. 3 (1967) pp. 171-82.

3. P. Yousif, "Le Symbolisme de la croix dans la nature chez Saint Ephrem," OCA, vol. 205, p. 215.

4. Nicene and Post-Nicene Fathers, p. 268.

5. Cited by Yousif, art. cit., p. 212.

6. R. Chesnut, Three Monophysite Christologies, pp. 117-35.

7. Nicene and Post-Nicene Fathers, pp. 306-7. See also: Yousif, art. cit., p. 221.

8. P. Yousif, "La Croix de Jesus et le Paradis d'Eden dans la typologie biblique de Saint Ephrem," Parole de l'Orient, vols. 6-7 (1975-6) p. 46.

9. Cited by S. Brock, "The Mysteries Hidden in the Side of Christ," Sobornost 7.6 (1978) pp. 463-7.

10. Yousif, "Le symbolisme...", pp. 218-9.

11. S. Brock, "Jacob of Serugh on the Veil of Moses," Sobornost, vol. 3 (1981) pp. 74-5. See also: D. O. Rousseau in his introduction to A. Raes, Le Mariage, sa célébration et sa spiritualité dans les Eglises d'O-rient (Editions de Chevetogne, 1958) pp. 13-6.

12. Cited by Brock, "Baptismal themes in the writings of Jacob of Serugh, Orientalia Christiana Analecta, vol. 205, pp.329-33.

13. Cited by Brock, "The Mysteries...", p. 468.

14. R. Murray, Symbols, pp. 323-4.

15. Yousif, "La Croix...", pp. 41-2.

16. Nicene and Post-Nicene Fathers, p. 212.

17. Brock, "The Mysteries...", p. 471.

18. Murray, Symbols, pp. 323-4.

19. Yousif, "La Croix...", p. 37.

20. Cited by Yousif, "Le Symbolisme...", p. 215, note 16. See also: p. 216, note 20.

21. T. Jansma, "Encore le credo de Jacques de Saroug," L'Orient Syrien, vol. 10 (1965) p. 336.

22. Brock, "Baptismal Themes...", p. 328.

23. Yousif, "La Croix...", p. 44.

24. J. Teixidor, "Le thème de la descente aux infers chez saint Ephrem," L'Orient Syrien, vol. 6 (1961) p. 26.

25. Nicene and Post-Nicene Fathers, p. 199.

26. Ibid., p. 306.

27. Ibid., p. 230.

28. Brock, Harp of the Spirit, p. 45.

29. Nicene and Post-Nicene Fathers, pp. 306-7.

30. Chesnut, op. cit., p. 117.

31. Nicene and Post-Nicene Fathers, p. 268.

32. Ibid., p. 205.

33. Brock, Harp, pp. 27-9.

34. Leonel L. Mitchell, "Four Fathers on Baptism: St. John Chrysostom, St. Ephraem, Theodore of Mopsuestia, Narsai," Studies on Syrain Baptismal Rites, ed. by Jacob Vellian, (Kottayam: C.M.S. Press, 1973) p. 52.

35. E. Khalifé-Hachem, "Office Maronite du Grand Dimanche de la Résurrection: Texte du Ramso et Commentaire," Parole de l'Orient, vol. 6-7 (1975-6) pp. 290-7.

36. Nicene and Post-Nicene Fathers, p. 216. See also: Hymns 54 and 61, Ibid., pp. 206, 213.

37. Ibid., p. 201.

38. Cited in Teixidor, art. cit., p. 37.

39. Chesnut, op. cit., pp. 127 ff.

40. Khalifé-Hachem, art. cit., p. 289.

41. Brock, Harp, pp. 66, 68.

42. T. Kronholm, Motifs, p. 42.

43. Brock, Harp, pp. 27-9.

44. Nicene and Post-Nicene Fathers, pp. 253-4.

45. Khalifé-Hachem, art. cit., p. 284.

46. R. Murray, "A Hymn of St. Ephrem to Christ," Sobornost 1.1 (1979) pp. 41, 46.

47. Nicene and Post-Nicene Fathers, p. 262.

48. Murray, "A Hymn of St. Ephrem to Christ," pp. 41-2, 47.

49. Brock, Harp, pp. 27 ff.

50. Nicene and Post-Nicene Fathers, p. 206.

51. S. Brock, "The Poetic Artistry of St. Ephrem: an analysis of H. Azym. III," Parole de l'Orient, vol. 6-7 (1975-6) pp. 23-4.

52. D. Outtier, "Contribution a l'étude de la Prehistoire des collections d'hymns d'Ephrem" Parole de l'Orient, vol. 6-7 (1975-6) p. 59.

53. Murray, "A Hymn of St. Ephrem to Christ," p. 41. See also: Nisibene Hymn, No. 66, Nicene and Post-Nicene Fathers, p. 218.

54. S. Brock, "Ephrem's Letter to Publius," Le Museon, vol. 89 (1976) pp. 278-80. See also: Hymn on the Nativity, No. 2, Nicene and Post-Nicene Fathers, p. 228.

# CHAPTER SIX

## DIVINIZATION AND THE HOLY SPIRIT

The process of divinization is rooted in the nature of creation, manifested in revelation, and reaches its fulness in the incarnation and redemption. The divinization of humans is the result of the work of redemption, and the active principle of divinization is the Holy Spirit. In the Syriac mind, all acts of power and sanctification are the work of the Spirit of God. This is especially highlighted in the 'epiklesis' which is an essential element of the Divine liturgy and the mysteries. While the Syriac writers reflect the New Testament references to the indwelling of all three Persons of the Trinity, the focus of attention for the work of divinization is the Holy Spirit.

Ephrem teaches that the purpose of the incarnation is the divinization of humans. In the Hymn on Virignity, No. 46, he says:

Liberty persuaded Adam to scorn his honor when he wished to become god while he was a creature. Grace purifies sin. God came, made himself man to save humanity from periditon. Behold the Son who purified the sin of the servant and made him divine as he desired.[1]

For Philoxenus of Mabboug, the basis for the presence of the Spirit of Christ in the baptized person is the fact that Christ assumed our common human nature. He declares:

The flesh which is common is his, and not the righteous alone, for he was enfleshed from the nature of humanity by means of the virgin, and became a man. Thus, he also dwells in all of us, in anyone willing to be baptised and born anew. "You are temples of God and the Spirit of God dwells in you." The Word dwells in us, therefore, by means of his Spirit. And our nature became a temple for him by means of his, having been emptied out and made flesh from us.[2]

Ephrem uses vivid imagery to express how Christ through his incarnation and Spirit brings about divinization. In his Hymn on the Faith, No. 10, he exclaims:

> When the Lord came down to earth, to mortals,
> a new creation he created them, like to the
> Watchers <the angels>.
> He mingled fire and spirit in them,
> to make them fire and spirit within.[3]

For the word "mingled" in the above passage, Ephrem
uses the Syriac term "mzag", which is Ephrem's term to
describe both the union of natures in Christ and our
union with him by grace and the mysteries <sacraments>.[4]

In his Hymn on the Faith, No. 18, Ephrem uses
the image of the wind and a sail with different
meanings. The wind refers to the Spirit and to divinity, while the sail refers to the body of Christ in
the womb of Mary and also to the altar linen as a sign
of the Eucharist. The thrust of the verse is to describe the sanctification of humans. Ephrem says:

> O sail, pure womb, symbol of the Body of our
> Redeemer!
> although filled with the wind, it by no means
> confines it;
> through the 'wind' dwelling in the 'sail'
> live the bodies wherein dwells the soul.[5]

The means of sanctification after the work of
Christ are the mysteries. As indicated above, the
Syriac fathers stress the presence of the Spirit in the
mysteries as the divinizing force. In his Hymn on the
Faith, No. 10, Ephrem establishes the role of the
Spirit, when he declares:

> Fire and the Spirit are in the womb of her who
> bore You,
> Fire and the Spirit are in the river in which
> you were baptized,
> Fire and the Spirit are in our baptism,
> and in the Bread and the Cup is Fire and the
> Holy Spirit.[6]

In the same hymn, Ephrem works on the image of fire to
express the sanctification of humans. He explains:

> Fire descended in wrath and consumed sinners;
> The fire of mercy descended and dwelt in the
> bread.

Instead of that fire which consumed mankind,
you have consumed Fire in the bread and you
have come to Life.[7]

In another hymn Ephrem further elaborates that that the
"Power of the Spirit who makes his place in the bread
enters to repose in us."[8]

Philoxenus of Mabboug speaks clearly about the
presence of the Word through the Spirit in the baptized. In the Monks of Senoun, he teaches that the
Holy Spirit dwells in us as God, because we have become
his temples. It is through baptism that we have received Christ who gives the Spirit. "...There, where
the Spirit is which he gives, in him also he dwells, by
his Spirit."[9]

In the Maronite liturgy, the prayer after the
'epiklesis' of the Anaphora of St. Cyril of Jerusalem
prays: "May the Holy Spirit purify and sanctify us.
May we share in His divinity and become sharers with
Him in the kingdom."

The Syriac fathers speak in intimate terms of
the presence of the Holy Spirit in the soul. Aphraat
in his Demonstration No. 6 on Monks warns that when the
Holy Spirit departs from a spirit, Satan draws near and
tries to cause him to sin so that the Holy Spirit might
leave altogether. He cautions that when the monk is
not fervent in the Spirit and his heart is inclining to
the thoughts of this world, he knows that the Spirit is
not with him. He should then pray and keep vigil that
the Spirit of God might come to him. Aphraat then
adds:

...They then that receive the Spirit of
Christ, come into the likeness of the heavenly
Adam, Who is our Saviour, our Lord Jesus
Christ. For the animal shall be swallowed up
in the spiritual, as I wrote unto thee above.
And the man that grieves the Spirit of Christ,
will be animal in the resurrection; because the
heavenly spirit is not within him that the
animal might be swallowed up in it.[10]

When Ephrem does speak of all three persons of
the Trinity, he relates their activity to a tripartite
view of humans, namely, that they are spirit, soul, and
body. In his Hymn on the Faith, No. 8, he explains:

The three Names are sown in three ways,
in the spirit, the soul and the body, mys-
teriously.
When this trinity within us is perfected by the
Three
it dominates even the sword!

If the spirit suffers, it is entirely imprinted
by the Father;
if the soul suffers, it is wholly mingled with
the Son;
and if the body is burnt in martyrdom,
then its communion with the Holy Spirit is com-
plete.[11]

Philoxenus of Mabboug develops a unique morality
based on the presence of the Holy Spirit in the soul.
He reasons that at baptism we receive the Holy Spirit,
not due to our justice, but to the grace of God.
Therefore, we cannot lose the Spirit by sin. What was
given as a gift, remains a gift. Philoxenus distinguishes between the sin which causes the death of
the soul, and the type of sin that does not separate us
completely from God. Apostacy belongs to the first
type, and by it we lose divine sonship and the Holy
Spirit which is its living manifestation. Only the
loss of faith kills the soul completely and causes the
loss of the Spirit. Philoxenus explains that sin as
such does not destroy the temple of God, just as a son
by sinning is not repudiated by his father even if he
offends him gravely. "Whatever are the sins and of-
fenses of a son, he does not lose his dignity of being
a son, to the point that the Father wishes to dis-
inherit him."[12]

Philoxenus raises the issue of how one could do
anything for salvation if he were not led by the
Spirit. He asks:

How dare we say: "Our Father who are in
heaven," when we approach the holy mysteries?
If the Spirit has abandoned us because of sin,
by what power do we call God our Father?"
...If he leaves us, how would we repent of our
sins? There is no penitence without the Holy
Spirit. And if he leaves us when we sin, who
arouses these sentiments in us? Perhaps, you
would say our will. And our will, who directs
it toward good? Who would aid it to do good?
Is it not the Holy Spirit?[13]

76

Reflecting the teaching of Ephrem, Philoxenus proceeds to respond to those who would raise the objection that the action of the Holy Spirit would take away freedom. Affirming that it is by freedom that we are in the image of God, Philoxenus explains that the Spirit does not act by violence to force the soul to do good, but He exhorts and attracts us. He takes an extremely benign view by saying that "neither adultery, nor thievery, nor fornication, nor false witness, nor any like action" is able to despoil us of our baptism and deprive us of the Holy Spirit. The sinner is an ill person and the Holy Spirit is his physician. It is he who arouses the sinner to repent and heals his sinfulness.[14]

## The Holy Spirit as Mother

Robert Murray and other writers observe that early Syriac writers understood the Holy Spirit in feminine terms. For Murray, the biblical roots of this idea may be the use of bird-imagery, especially when one considers that the Semetic verbal root "rhp" used in speaking of the Spirit, also has the meaning of a mother bird hovering. For example, Genesis 1, 2 speaks of the spirit of God hovering over the face of the waters. This Old Testament image may be reflected in the Spirit as a dove over the waters of the baptism of Jesus. Aphraat tells us that we should adore God as Father and the Holy Spirit as mother. For Murray, this may be simply attributing to the Holy Spirit the motherly character which the later parts of Isaiah (49, 14-5; 66, 13) find in God. While Ephrem conjugates the word for spirit as feminine, he seems only once to refer to actual femininity.[15]

# Notes to Chapter Six

1. G. Saber, La Theologie Baptismale de Saint Ephrem, p. 121.

2. R. Chesnut, Three Monophysite Christologies, p. 84.

3. R. Murray, "A Hymn of St. Ephrem to Christ on the Incarnation, the Holy Spirit, and the Sacraments," Eastern Churches Review, vol. 3 (1970-1) p. 143.

4. Ibid., p. 147.

5. Peter Yousif, "St. Ephrem on Symbols in Nature: Faith, the Trinity and the Cross (Hymn on the Faith, No. 18)," Eastern Churches Quarterly, vol. 10 (1978) pp. 54, 58-59.

6. S. Brock, Harp of the Spirit, p. 16.

7. R. Murray, art. cit., pp. 143-4.

8. F. Graffin, "L'Eucharistie chez Saint Ephrem," Parole de l'Orient, vol. 4 (1973) pp. 100-5.

9. Chesnut, op. cit., p. 84.

10. Nicene and Post-Nicene Fathers, pp. 373-4.

11. Yousif, art. cit., p. 53.

12. P. Harb, "L'évolution de la morale dans l'église syrienne," Parole de l'Orient, vol. 1 (1970) pp. 45-6.

13. Ibid., p. 47.

14. Ibid., pp. 47-8.

15. R. Murray, Symbols of Church and Kingdom, pp. 313-9.

# CHAPTER SEVEN

## THE CHURCH

The Church is primarily the vehicle whereby new members of Christ are formed. It is the source of the mysteries <sacraments> through which sanctification occurs. Early Syriac thought still awaiting an imminent 'parousia' did not concern itself with the structural make-up of the Chruch. Also, it is only when serious threats of heresy began to develop in the fourth century on that questions of the unity and cohesiveness of the Church became important. A prominent theme in Syriac writings is that God has rejected the chosen people of the Old Testament in favor of the 'Church of the Nations'. As we have seen, this new Church is betrothed by Christ at his Baptism in the Jordan and is wedded to Christ on the cross. The blood and water from the side of Christ represent the mysteries of 'Initiation' by which members of the Church are incorporated and nourished.

One limitation on Ephrem's ecclesiology is the fact that he probably did not have first hand knowledge of all the books of the New Testament. He was familiar with the Diatesseron, Acts, St. Paul's epistles, and the apocryphal Third Corinthians.[1] The probability that he did not know I Peter could have hindered the development of a full ecclesiology. Also, the Syriac Church received the book of Revelation at a comparatively late date. R. Murray believes that even the Syriac reference to a heavenly Jerusalem is an allusion to Galatians 4, 26.[2]

For Ephrem the Church is first a local Christian community such as the Church of Nisibis or of Edessa. In addition, the Church is the great Christian community instituted by Christ in place of the synagogue. It is the refound Paradise, the Body of Christ, and his holy and immacualte spouse.[3]

On the other hand, it is possible that the strong ascetical spirit of the early Syriac Church with its corresponding eschatological expectation could have diminished the role of the Church in the world in their thinking. For Aphraat, Ephrem, and the Liber Graduum, the 'kingdom' is almost an exclusively eschatological conception, not yet realized.[4]

The image of Church as mother, rare in earlier documents, is developed by Ephrem in the sense that both Mary and the Church are seen as the second Eve. Only the Liber Graduum makes much of the Church as mother.[5]

## The Church of the Nations

The predominant theme of the fourth century fathers is that the chosen people have been replaced by a "new people", the 'nation from the nations', the Church of the Gentiles. For Aphraat, the significance of Abraham is that God promised to extend salvation through him to all nations. The faith of Abraham reveals that in the future, any person of any nation can be saved. As an instrument of this plan of universal salvation, God chose one people for his own, but all its rites were types seeking fulfillment in the Church. Ephrem in his <u>Hymn on the Unleavened Bread, No. 5,</u> says: "The type was in Egypt, the reality in the Church; the sealing of the reward <will be> in the kingdom." For Aphraat, the Church is the new circumcision, new Passover, new covenant, but especially a new spirit, a spirit of freedom.[6]

This theme is reflected in the Maronite liturgy. The 'anamnesis' of the Anaphora of St. Cyril of Jerusalem prays: "...Let the light of your face shine upon us, the Church which you chose from among the nations..." The 'prayer of forgiveness' of the Dedication of the Church Sunday declares: "...He summons distant peoples to her and He collects the scattered nations into her..."

## The Body of Christ

Ephrem sets up an implicit basis for the Church when he teaches that the same body of Christ that healed us and rose again, has been given to us in sacramental form to heal us and incorporate us in him in the Church, and gives us a pledge of the resurrection.[7] In his <u>Commentary on the Diatesseron</u>, Ephrem explains:

If then the Chruch is his body, as Paul his witness said, believe that his Church has passed through all this without corruption. Just as by the condemnation of the one Adam all bodies died and must die, so by the victory of this one body of Christ, the whole Church found life and lives. But just as, because the bodies which themselves have sinned, themselves must also die, and the earth their mother was cursed, so because of this body, because it is itself the Church, which is not corrupted, its earth was blessed from the beginning. For the earth is the body of Mary, the temple which received the seed.[8]

Another image which develops the idea of Body of Christ is that of Christ as vine and vineyard. Through the use of this imagery, Ephrem speaks of the Church as the Body of Christ, one with him as he is with his Father. He is one yet many in his members. This is expressed in images such as Christ is the vineyard and Christians are vines in him, and where he is the branch of the vine and Christians are fruits hanging on him; and where as vine or especially as olive, he is the 'tree of life', source of sacramental grace for the Chruch.[9]

Nevertheless, R. Murray concludes that fourth century Syriac literature did not develop much the ideas of corporate personality and Mystical Body. Neither Aphraat nor Ephrem seem to start from St. Paul. They seem to center mainly on the personal body of Christ.[10]

James of Serug uses the Syraic term "to mix" to describe the union between Christ and the Church. He uses the same idea to describe the relationship between Christ and the bread and wine of the Eucharist. He declares that Christ, the rich bridegroom, and the Church, the poor bride, are made one. James says that Christ came to "take the Church and mix it with his body and make it from him, and the two of them would be one...the groom from the virgin and the bride from Baptism." R. Chesnut concludes that it is unclear whether the Church comes to belong to Jesus as an extension of his own body, or whether they are to be 'one' in the way in which any husband and wife are one.[11]

## Betrothed in the Jordan and from the side of Christ

The Syriac mind views the Church itself in sacramental terms. The Church is not only the source of the mysteries, but is a sacrament of the union of Christ with his people. As we have already seen, the origins of the Church are traced to the baptism of Christ and his death on the cross. The baptism of

Christ in the Jordan is a key event, which also was
foreshadowed in the Old Testament with events that took
place at the well. In his <u>Hymn on the Ephiphany, No.
8</u>, Ephrem explains:

> At the well Rebecca received in her ears and
> hands the jewels. The Spouse of Christ put on
> precious things that are from the water: on her
> hand the living Body, and in her ears the pro-
> mises.[12]

In his <u>Commentary on the Diatesseron</u>, Ephrem
cites various betrothals that took place at the well,
such as Eleazer (for Isaac) with Rebecca, Jacob with
Rachel, and Moses with Zipporah: "All these were types
of Our Lord who espoused his Church at this baptism in
the Jordan."[13]

In <u>Hymn on the Epiphany, No. 14</u>, Ephrem presents
Jesus as reflecting on his baptism at the Jordan:

> My thought bore me to Jordan, and I saw
> a marvel when there was revealed the glorious
> Bridegroom who to the Bride shall bring freedom
> and holiness.
> . . .
> The Bride you betrothed to me awaits me,
> that I should go down, be baptised, and sanc-
> tify her.
> . . .
> The waters in my Baptism are sanctified,
> and fire and the Spirit from Me shall they re-
> ceive.[14]

The Church soiled by sin was in need of purification which happened in Baptism, which in turn owes
its redemptive force to the death of Christ on the
cross. The baptism of Christ in the Jordan is the betrothal of the Church. After her purification by the
heavenly spouse, the Church is without stain and beautiful, richly decked out in an inconceivable brightness.[15]

The baptism in the Jordan reaches its climax
with the salvific death of Christ on the cross. From
the side of Christ comes blood and water which effect
the birth of the Church, and also her wedding to her
heavenly groom. James of Serug describes Christ as
offering his suffering as a dowry for the Church, his
spouse, and also Christ is a shepherd who leads his

flock by his staff, the cross:

> Yes, the Son of God gave his sufferings by love so to espouse, by the price of his pains, the abandoned Church.
> For this adorer of idols, he suffers on the cross, so that after his sufferings she was all holy to him.
> He accepted to lead to pasture all the flock of men, with the great staff of the crucifixion in suffering.
> Nations, worlds, classes, crowds, and peoples, He accepts to lead all, to have in return only the Church.[16]

The Maronite liturgy reflects the theme of the wedding of the Church to Christ on the cross in many places. The "etro" <prayer of incense> of the Evening Office of Easter Thursday says of the Church: "Your Chruch, O Christ, who on the cross has come out of the wound from your side, as Eve had come out of the side of Adam in paradise..." The Eucharistic aspect is seen in the 'prayer of forgiveness' of the Evening Office of the First Sunday of Lent: "Praise, glory, and honor to the spouse of the Church who has united her to him in his blood, delivering to her his holy body..." These themes are re-echoed in the 'prayer of forgiveness' of the Consecration of the Church Sunday: "...through the death of the bridegroom she was betrothed. Thus was she crowned with thorns, and through the passion she was redeemed. Adorned with fine robes, she arose in divine glory as a well-appointed palace, a firmly set city, a fortified tower, and a holy mountain."

Both the East and West Syriac liturgies compare the union of Christ with his Church to the marriage union of man and woman. The Maronite ritual on marriage reflects a developed theology of the Church. The 'prayer of forgiveness' declares: "May we be worthy to raise glory to the heavenly spouse....In his love, He has acquired the Church of the Nations, and by his cross, has washed and purified her, and made her his glorious spouse. He has invited to his marriage prophets, apostles, and holy martyrs..." The "qolo" hymn adds: "Alleluia, there was not in this world and there would never be a Spouse as the one who was acquired by the Christ-Groom. Her beauty surpasses all beauty and the Spouse who has married her is unable to die. From the blood which came from his side, He wrote her dowry."[17]

This theme of the wedding of the Church to Christ is found developed in other Churches of the Syriac tradition. W. de Vries writing on the Nestorian tradition summarizes his findings regarding its ecclesiology as teaching that the heavenly Father has chosen the Church from among the nations as a bride for his Son. Christ acquires his betrothed at the price of his sacrificed body and poured blood. The moment of betrothal is sometimes the crucifixion, sometimes the baptism in the Jordan. To be purified the Church had to receive the waters of baptism. The Redemption primarily through the death on the cross has liberated the Church from the bonds of Satan. Among the presents Christ gives his betrothed are his Body and Blood and the rebirth of Baptism.[18]

R. Murray expands the relationship of the Church to Christ on the cross, by studying the imagery of the cross as 'tree'. Therefore, the Church is one with Christ as Mystic Vineyard, Vine and Grape, and receives from Christ the oil of initiation, consecration and healing from him as Mystic Olive.[19]

## Incorporation by the Spirit

In the view of Philoxenus of Mabboug, Baptism grafts new members into Christ because the "Spirit is mixed there"; and if new members receive life and power and become "living members", it is because they have been created by the Spirit as new persons. The Church is born from baptism, but baptism is the Spirit[20] Narsai in his 17th Homily declares: "We confess the one Church, sanctified by the Holy Spirit." [21]

## The Eucharist and the Church

As we have noted above, the body of Christ by which he healed humanity and rose again, he gave us in sacramental form to incorporate us in him in the Church.[22] Ephrem in his Hymn on Paradise, No. 6, proclaims:

In the Church he set the Word,
which causes joy by its promises
and fear by its threats.
The assembly of the saints
is a symbol of paradise.
The fruit of him who gives life to all
is picked in her every day.

In her, my brethern, are pressed
the grapes of him who is the Medicine of Life.[23]

Sebastian Brock believes the Church should be
viewed in a two-fold aspect: on the one hand, it manifests itself in the sacraments, as Baptism and the
Eucharist; on the other hand, it represents the to-
tality of its individual members. The Church, as the
vehicle of the sacraments, is the means of the sanctification of the Church, as the assembly of individual
members.[24]

## The Church as Rock

A favorite Syriac theme is that the Church is
established on faith. Reflecting various Biblical
images, the Church is seen as built on the rock of
faith and that the Church is itself a building. According to Aphraat, Christ the chief shepherd made
Simon the chief shepherd in his place. Christ was the
"kepha" <rock> foretold by prophecy and type, and made
Simon the "kepha" in his place. He said that on that
"kepha" he would build his Church, and the "bars of
sheol" would be powerless against it. The "kepha" is
the foundation of the Church, and therefore a functional title given by Christ to Simon.

In Demonstration, No. 1, Aphraat explains that
the "building" is the structure of faith laid on the
foundation of Christ the firm Rock. "When the whole
building has gone up and is finished and perfected, it
becomes a house and temple for the indwelling of
Christ." Aphraat applies the figure of rock as foundation to both Christ and Peter. The building on the
rock is normally faith, but it is also Peter and sometimes the Apostles (James and John are "pillars"). The
Church is the "One House" and Christians are the
temples of the Spirit.[25]

Ephrem's development is similar to that of Aphraat. Christ is the rock or stone, prefigured by a
number of types. The theme of Christ the rock making
Simon the rock is often implicit, but rarely explicit
as in Aphraat. Simon's name "kepha" is once again seen
as a functional title shared with Christ.[26]

The Maronite liturgy offers a similar interpretation of the Biblical passages. The prayer after
the 'epiklesis' in the Anaphora of St. James petitions

for "...strength for your Holy Church which you founded
on the rock of faith, so that the power of evil shall
not prevail against her..." The "mazmoro" verse for
the Consecration of the Church Sunday prays: "The Lord
built his Holy Church as a rock of faith. Simon Peter
entered and laid the foundations and Paul adorned the
building."

## The Church of Truth

As we have noted, the Syriac fathers in the
early centuries had a sacramental view of the Church
and concentrated on its local structures. As time went
on, the Church as communtiy was seen as the body of
truth, and heresy represented a threat to unity.
Ephrem in his Hymn against Heresies, No. 2, exclaims:

> This is the body of truth, whose words
> the foolish and erring have cut up like limbs;
> whereas, since it is spiritual
> it is found to be whole and entire.
> . . .
> But in the Church of the Truth
> it \<truth\> is perfect, and perfects her.
> . . .
> It is thy joy, O Church, this body of truth
> ordered in its members, concordant in its
> words,
> faithful in its promises, crowned in its tri-
> umphs.

And in his Hymn on the Faith, No. 52, he prays:

> ...that from all churches there may be a
> single Church of Truth...[27]

According to W. de Vries, from the first centuries up to the Arab invasion, the concept of "communion" \<"sawtofuto"\> is in the first rank. Communion
is a sacramental-juridical bond which ties the members
of the true Church of Christ, to the exclusion of all
others. Ecclesiastical authority is the judge of who
belongs to this communion, of which the conclusive sign
is the Eucharistic celebration. Since heretics were
excluded, the preliminary requirement of communion is
true faith. True faith is general accord with the
bishops and faithful, and when this accord is dubious,
is the teaching of the Fathers of the primitive Church,
and of the Apostles and Scripture.[28]

In regard to the authority in the Church, the
Syriac fathers speak about Christ sharing his functions
with humans. According to R. Murray, the apostolic
ministry shares in Christ's function as Head of the
Body, as Spouse of the Bride, as Priest and keybearer,
shepherd, steward, farmer, physician. Christ's work as
witness, healer, guide and helper continues in the
sacramental society of the Church, though only by
"under-shepherds" and "under-stewards", who must always
remember that they have an account to render.[29]

# Notes to Chapter Seven

1. Robert Murray, "St. Ephrem the Syrian on Church Unity," Eastern Churches Quarterly, vol. 15 (1963) p. 168.

2. Robert Murray, Symbols of Church and kingdom, pp. 20-21.

3. G. Saber, La Theologie baptismale de Saint Ephrem, p. 51.

4. Murray, op. cit., p. 346.

5. Ibid., p. 157.

6. Ibid., pp. 41-61.

7. Ibid., pp. 69-72.

8. Ibid., pp. 83-4.

9. Ibid., pp. 113, 129-30.

10. Ibid., pp. 93-4.

11. Roberta Chesnut, Three Monophysite Christologies, p. 134.

12. Nicene and Post-Nicene Fathers, p. 275.

13. Murray, op. cit, p. 135.

14. Nicene and Post-Nicene Fathers, pp. 284-5.

15. William de Vries, "La Conception de l'Église chez les Jacobites," L'Orient Syrien, vol. 2 (1957) pp. 113-4.

16. F. Graffin, "Recherches sur le thème de l'église-épouse dans les liturgies et litterature patristique de langue syriaque," L'Orient Syrien, vol. 3 (1958) p. 331.

17. Jeanne-Ghislaine Van Overstraeten, "Les Liturgies Nuptiales des Églises de Langue Syriaque et le Mystère de l'Église-Épouse," Parole de l'Orient, vol. 8 (1977-8) pp. 296-9.

18. W. de Vries, "La Conception de l'Église chez les Nestoriens," L'Orient Syrien, vol. 3 (1958) pp. 163-4.

19. Murray, op. cit., p. 342.

20. P. Harb, "La conception pneumatologique chez Philoxene de Mabbug," Melto, vol. 5 (1969) pp. 5-6.

21. W. de Vries, "La conception...chez les Nestoriens," p. 163.

22. Murray, op. cit., pp. 69-70.

23. Ibid., pp. 128-9.

24. S. Brock, "The Mysteries Hidden in the Side of Christ," Sobornost, 7.6 (1978) pp. 469-70.

25. R. Murray, "The Rock and the House on the Rock," Orientalia Christiana Periodica, vol. 30, pp. 315-24.

26. Ibid., pp. 325-50.

27. Cited by Murray, "St. Ephrem.." pp. 168, 175.

28. de Vries, "La conception...chez les Jacobites," pp. 116-24.

29. Murray, op. cit., pp. 158, 204.

CHAPTER EIGHT

MARY

As we have seen, the Syriac writers claimed that Christ throughout his life on earth was also continually the divine presence, possessing the power of creation and annihilation, and the healing power of redemption. In their minds the mother who conceived and bore him would be intimately affected and divinized by that power. However, Mary was also very much a human possessed of free will. Through her virginity and free assent to the will of the Father, she takes away the shame of her own ancient mother Eve, and in so doing becomes the first member of the Church. It was natural for Syriac writers to see Mary as the fulfillment of Old Testament types, and a symbol of the future Church.

James of Serug celebrates Mary's purity as a fitting dwelling for the presence of God. In his metric homilies, he declares: "God sees her, He sees the purity and transparence of her soul and he wishes to make his dwelling in that which has been purified from all sin." [1]

## The Holy Spirit and Mary

In the mind of Ephrem, as we have seen, the Holy Spirit is the principle of divinization. The 'epiklesis' of the Spirit occurred not only in the baptism of Christ in the Jordan, but also continues in the mysteries of Baptism and the Eucharist. However, the same action of the Spirit took place in the womb of Mary, as we have already noted in the chapter on divinization. In the Hymn on the Faith, No. 10, he declares:

In the womb that bore you are Fire and the Spirit,
Fire and Spirit are in the river where you were baptized,
Fire and Spirit are in our Baptism too,
And in the Bread and the Cup are Fire and Spirit.

Moses Bar Kepha (+903) in his commentary on the liturgy notes the significance by saying that just as the Holy Spirit descended on the womb of Mary and made a body for God the Word from the flesh of the Virgin,

91

so the Spirit descends on the bread and wine on the altar and makes them into the Body and Blood of God the Word which originated from the Virgin.[2]

Sebastian Brock dwells on the meaning of this parallelism between the Annunciation and the Eucharist. For him the 'epiklesis' of the Holy Spirit effects a new relationship of the created world to the Creator. The bread and wine which represent both 'fruit of the earth' and 'the work of human hands' are transformed into the saving body and blood of Christ. This perhaps indicates how the Holy Spirit can transform the material world into sacrament. He cites Philoxenus as saying (Homily 3, 53): "...without faith, everything is ordinary; but when faith has come, even mean things appear glorious."[3]

S. Brock also explains that according to an ancient myth, it was when lightning struck the pearl oyster in the sea that pearls were created -- the result of two disparate elements, fire and water. In his hymns on the faith 81-85, Ephrem meditates on the mystery of the birth of Christ the pearl as a result of the coming of the fire of the Holy Spirit upon the 'watery tomb' of Mary.[4]    In the first Hymn on the Pearl, Ephrem declares: "It is again Mary that I discern and her pure conception. The Church also and the Son in her womb as the cloud that carried Him: Symbol of heaven and where His resplendent light radiates."[5]

Besides the sanctifying presence of the Holy Spirit, Ephrem believed that it was the presence of the Word in Mary's womb that sanctified her. In his Hymn on the Church, No. 36, Ephrem meditates on the effects of the presence of Christ the Light had on his mother Mary:

> As though on an eye
> the Light settled in Mary,
> It polished her mind,
> made bright her thought
> and pure her understanding,
> causing her virginity to shine.
> ...
> As the Daystar in the river,
> the Bright One in the tomb,
> he shone forth on the mountain top
> and gave brightness too in the womb;
> he dazzled as he went up from the river,
> gave illumination at his ascension.

The brightness which Moses put on
was wrapped on him from without,
whereas the river in which Christ was baptized
put on Light from within,
and so did Mary's body, in which he resided,
gleam from within.
Just as Moses gleamed
with divine glory
because he saw the splendor briefly,
how much more should the body
wherein Christ resided gleam,
and the river where he was baptized?[6]

As we have indicated before, for Ephrem and the
Syriac fathers creation itself prepares progressively
for the coming of Christ through symbol and image. In
this view Mary occupies the climactic role of creation.
We repeat a citation from his Hymn on Virginity, No. 5:

Creation traced the symbols of Christ; Mary
fashioned his limbs; it was many wombs that
engendered the only-begotten Son -- for his
mother's womb gave birth to his humanity, while
creation gave symbolic birth to him.[7]

### Mary and Eve

The Syriac fathers in meditating on Mary focus
on the central event of the Annunciation. An advanced
theology of Mary is achieved by contrasting the effect
of sin brought about by Eve's failure and the redemption achieved through the free co-operation of
Mary. This theme is seen in the metric homilies of
James of Serug when he declares: "From the silence of
Eve came defeat and dishonor; from the words of Mary,
Life, Light and victory."[8]

Ephrem in his Commentary on the Diatesseron uses
multiple images to show that the sin that occurred in
Paradise is overcome by Mary at the Annunciation, and
by her son on the cross:

Death entered by the ear of Eve; therefore life
entered by the ear of Mary. By the wood of the
tree man came to be a debtor; therefore when
the Lord came he paid the debt by the wood of
the Cross.[9]

Ephrem further relates Mary to the 'robe of

glory', the image of sanctification that Adam and Eve lost. In his <u>Hymn on the Nativity, No. 17</u>, he explains:

> In her virginity leaves of shame
> did Eve put on; your Mother put on
> in her virginity a robe of glory,
> sufficient for all. "A little cloak,
> The body, I gave to the clother of all."[10]

James of Serug in his metric homilies expands on these themes of Ephrem. He adds the idea that Mary undoes the harm incurred by her aged mother Eve. He explains:

> The second Eve has given birth to Life, among mortals;
> She has removed the debt contracted by Eve, her mother.
> The young daughter <Mary> has given her hand and brought help to her aged mother <Eve> buried in the earth;
> She has raised her from the fall caused by the Serpent.
> This was the daughter <Mary> who wove the robe of glory and gave it to her father <Adam> who covered his body which had remained naked since the Tree of the temptation.[11]

As we have seen, the Syriac tradition describes the state of sin in the world as darkness. Light is not only the image of God but the instrument of victory over sin. Ephrem in contrasting Eve and Mary also develops imagery regarding darkness and light. In the <u>Hymn on the Church, No. 37</u>, he says:

> The world, you see, has two eyes fixed in it;
> Eve was its left, blind,
> while the right eye, bright, is Mary.
> Through the eye that was darkened the whole world was darkened,
> and men groped and thought that every stone that they stumbled upon was a god, calling falsehood truth.
> But when the world was illumined by that other eye and the heavenly Light
> that resided in its midst, men became reconciled once again with God,
> realizing that what they stumbled on was destroying their very life.[12]

Ephrem expands this contrast between Eve and Mary, and applies it to the Eucharist. In his <u>Hymn on the Unleavened Bread, No. 6</u>, he declares: "Mary has given us the Bread of rest in place of the bread of toil which Eve provided."[13]

Besides the contrasts already mentioned, other parallels are that while Eve was wounded by the serpent, Mary and her son defeated him. As Eve was the mother that brought death unto her children, Mary is the second life-giving mother of humanity, and her offspring, 'the medicine of life', is the antidote to the 'drug of death' through which Eve was poisoned.[14]

The Syriac writers contrast Mary not only with Eve, but also with other facets of the original paradise including Adam, the tree, and the earth itself. In his <u>Hymn on the Nativity, No. 1</u>, Ephrem speaks about the "virgin earth" that gave birth to Adam who was "lord of the earth" and at the nativity, another virgin gives birth to the "Adam who is the Lord of heaven."[15] Ephrem expands this theme by incorporating it into the Pauline reference to death coming through the first Adam. We repeat here part of a citation from his <u>Commentary on the Diatesseron</u> we made in the chapter on the Church:

...But just as because the bodies which themselves have sinned, themselves must also die, and the earth their mother was cursed, so because this body, because it itself is the Church, which is not corrupted, the earth was blessed from the beginning. For the earth is the body of Mary, the temple which recieved the seed."[16]

James of Serug finds direct parallels between Adam and Mary, especially by contrasting the origin of Eve with the virginal conception of Mary. In his metric homilies he explains that just as Adam gave birth to Eve without sexual relations, so Mary gave birth in similar fashion. The Spirit breathed on the face of Adam and he gave birth to Eve, so the same Spirit was received by Mary and she gave birth to her Son. In Adam's giving birth to the 'mother of all the living', we have a prefiguring of the birth of Christ, the source of all life.[17]

James of Serug goes further and attributes an

95

active role to Mary in the work of Redemption:

> Thanks to Mary, the road toward Eden which had
> been closed was able to be trod upon anew,
> the serpent has fled and humans are able to go
> to God,
> thanks to Mary, the cherubim has turned away
> his sword,
> renouncing the guarding of the Tree of Life
> \<Christ\> who henceforth is given as nour-
> ishment.[18]

The Maronite liturgy in the Evening Office for
Mary proclaims: "You resemble, Mary, the paradise where
was planted the tree of life, you from whom appeared
the Creator and giver of life. Paradise however has
given to humanity the fruit of sin which corrupted the
human race in its root, but, you, you have given the
blessed fruit who has saved the whole human race, and
has given it the life of grace."

### Other types and symbols of Mary

The Syriac writers employed various images in
trying to comprehend the meaning of Mary's role. In
the Hymn on Mary, No. 7, attributed to Ephrem, Mary is
described as a ship who bears the "great steersman of
creation" who brought peace to heaven and earth.[19] In
a Homily on the Nativity also attributed to Ephrem,
Mary is compared to the 'burning bush'. He declares
that it is amazing how the womb of Mary was able to
carry "flaming fire" and not be burnt. It must be compared to the bush on Horeb which "bore God in the
flame".[20] In the same Homily, several titles of Mary
are listed:

> The titles of Mary are many
> and it is right that I should use them:
> she is the palace where dwells
> the mighty King of kings;
> . . .
> Again, she is the new heaven,
> in which there dwells the King of kings;
> He shone out in her and came forth into crea-
> tion,
> formed and clothed in her features.
> She is the stem of the cluster of grapes,
> she gave forth fruit beyond nature's means,
> and He, though His nature bore no resemblance
> to her,

96

put on her hue and came forth from her,
She is the spring, whence flowed
living water for the thirsty,
and those who have tasted its draft
give forth fruit a hundred fold. [21]

Sebastian Brock observes that the Syriac writers saw
many Biblical types of Mary, but the great majority of
them such as ark, burning bush, temple, all have in
common the fact that they contained or carried something holier than themselves. [22]

## Mary's relationship to Christ

Ephrem further develops Mary's role in salvation
by meditating on the various ways that Mary is related
to Christ. In his Hymn on the Nativity, No. 16, he has
her speaking:

How shall I call you, O stranger to us,
Who became one of us? Shall I call you 'Son'?
Shall I call you 'Brother'? Shall I call you
'Bridegroom'?
Shall I call you 'Lord'? Begetter of his mother
By a second birth from out of the waters!

For I am your sister of the house of David
who is our second father; and yet I am your
mother
because of your conception; and I am <your>
Bride
because of your chastity: Handmaid and daughter
by blood and water, for you have bought and
baptized <me>

The Son of the Most High came to dwell in me
and I became his mother, And as I bore him,
by another birth he in turn bore me,
by a second birth. The robe of his mother
which he put on, his body, I have put on its
glory! [23]

Ephrem puts these thoughts more succinctly in the Hymn
on the Nativity, No. 11, when he says: "She alone is
Your mother, but she is Your sister with everyone else.
She was Your mother, she was your sister, she was your
bride too along with all chaste souls. You, who are
Your mother's beauty, Yourself adorned her with everything." [24]

# Notes to Chapter Eight

1. S. Brock, "Marie dans la tradition Syriaque," _Letter de Ligugé_, vol. 189 (1978) p. 6.

2. S. Brock, "Mary and the Eucharist: an oriental perspective," _Sobornost_, 1:2 (1979) p. 51.

3. _Ibid._, p. 53.

4. _Ibid._, p. 56

5. F. Graffin, "Les Hymnes sur la perle de saint ephrem," _L'Orient Syrien_, vol. 12 (1967) p. 133.

6. S. Brock, "St. Ephrem on Christ as Light in Mary and in the Jordan: _Hymni De Ecclesia 36_," _Eastern Churches Review_, vol. 7 (1975) p. 138.

7. S. Brock, _Harp of the Spirit_, p. 13

8. S. Brock, "Marie dans la tradition...," p. 6.

9. R. Murray, "Mary, the Second Eve in the Early Syriac Fathers," _Eastern Chruches Review_, vol. 3 (1970-1) p. 374.

10. _Ibid._, p. 376.

11. Brock, "Marie dans la tradition...," p. 11.

12. S. Brock, "The Poet as Theologian," _Sobornost_, 7.4 (1977) p. 248.

13. Brock, "Mary and the Eucharist," p. 57.

14. Kronholm, _Motifs from Genesis 1-11..._, pp. 105-6.

15. Brock, "Marie dans la tradtion...," p. 9.

16. Murray, "Mary, the Second Eve...," p. 380.

17. Brock, "Marie dans la tradition...," pp. 9-10.

18. _Ibid._, p. 12.

19. Brock, _The Harp of the Spirit_, p. 60.

20. Ibid., p. 63.

21. Ibid., pp. 67-8. James of Serug echoes the image of Mary as a 'well': "Mary is the 'new well' whence flowed the living waters; though unpierced she gave birth to abundant streams for the thirsty world." S. Brock, "The Mysteries Hidden in the Side of Christ," p. 470.

22. Brock, Harp, p. 34; and "Marie dans la tradition...," p. 9.

23. Murray, "Mary, the Second Eve...," p. 376.

24. Brock, Harp, p. 35.

CHAPTER NINE

MYSTERIES OF INITIATION, Part 1

## Baptism and Chrismation

The Incarnation and Redemption of Christ represent the fulfillment of creation and the realization of the shadows and types of the Old Testament. However, Christ not only brings the completion of salvation but the reality of the divinization of creatures, primarily through the action of the Spirit. The events of Christ's Baptism in the Jordan and his death on the cross were not meant to be distinct moments in time, but manifest a power that will extend through time. The waters blessed by the Baptism of Christ and the blood and water which poured from the side of Christ are gifts to his Bride the Church and her children through history. While the types have been fulfilled, the new "mysteries" have been established with divinizing power by the symbolic actions of Christ.

The central mystery is the Eucharist which is both the cause and sign of Church community. In fact, the assmebly partaking of the Eucharist is the essential core of what Church is. However, it is only those who have been delivered by the divinizing power of Christ's Spirit in the waters of Baptism and the anointing of Chrism are in a position to partake of the Eucharist. According to P. Verghese, the Eucharist is the 'raison d'etre' of the body of Christ in the world of space and time. All "mysteries" are completed in the Eucharist.[1] The mysteries of Baptism, Chrismation, and Eucharist are integral elements in the process of divinization.

Before discussing the mysteries individually, some further observations should be made regarding the meaning of 'mystery' itself in the Syriac tradition. As we have noted above, the Syriac term for mystery is "raza", and in the fourth century it had various applications. It was used for any religious symbol (especially Old Testament 'types'), for sacramental rites, and in the plural for the Eucharist.[2]

P. Verghese explains that "raza" in Syriac comes from the root "raz" meaning to conspire, and might have had its origin in the mystery cults. But, in ecclesiastical Syria, it came to have a special meaning of an act of the chosen community, or instructing the baptized, or performing the great mystery of the upper room. A mystery can thus show forth some event of eternal significance. Also, the "mystery" is a corporate act of a specific body, and is closed to those outside it. It is, so to speak, a reality of the eternal order, manifesting itself in time, through a visible corporate action of the Church, to those already initiated into the mystery and living by it.[3]

W. de Vries adds that the idea of mystery conveys the meaning of "mysterious symbols" of a superior world, which are able to introduce us in an efficacious way to that world. It is especially clear that the water of Baptism, Chrism, and the Eucharist are made up of matter informed by spirit. The Fathers describe the action of the Spirit as "hovering" or "brooding" over the matter. The divine is thereby concretized and incorporated in visible matter. For example, Moses Bar Kepha draws a parallel between the Eucharist and Chrism: "We understand and we concieve with the eyes of the soul God the Word who unites himself with bread and wine and with the oil of chrism."[4] Narsai stresses the relationship of the visible oil and water to the inward actions of Christ and the Spirit. "By outward things, God gives assurance of his works done in secret."[5] In the Syriac liturgical tradition, the water of baptism, the bread and wine of the Eucharist, and chrism are all three consecrated by an 'epiklesis'. They become "dynamized" matter.

J. Lecuyer sees this view of mystery reflected in the liturgy. He explains that at the beginning of the anaphora, the faithful are to believe that beyond sensible appearances and the terrestrial signs of the liturgy, there is an invisible and celestial reality that is being accomplished. Every mystery is the indication in signs and symbols of invisible and ineffable things. For John Chrysostom, if the Eucharist is a sacrifice which is accomplished on earth, the reality which it contains is all celestial. "To assist at the sacrifice is to asist at a celestial spectacle." Our altar is a celestial table, which recieves gifts of the earth and on which is operated an admirable exchange between earth and heaven; it has a double presence: "fixed on the earth, it is near the celestial throne."[6]

## Baptism

The Syriac church considers the Baptism

of Christ to be the central event that established the mystery of Baptism. Through Baptism in the Jordan River, Christ consecrated all the rivers of the world. The fulfillment of Christ's baptismal action takes place on the cross, when blood and water flow from the side of Christ. However, the earliest tradition did not stress the idea of 'dying and rising' concerning Baptism, but rather, Baptism as a new womb giving birth to new children bearing the image of the New Adam and being vested again in the "robe of glory". Baptism reverses the sad events of Paradise.

### The Baptism in the Jordan

Speaking about the Syriac tradition, S. Brock says that the baptism of Christ was the source of Christian baptism. At his Baptism, there is the public proclamation of his Sonship <Mark 1, 11>. Even in the New Testament, it seems that Christ's baptism was regarded as 'anointing' <Acts 10, 38; see: Lk 4, 18>, and the choice of Psalm 2, 7 provided a basis for Jesus' baptism as his public anointing as Messiah-king.[7]

Ephrem views the baptism of Christ in the water as analogous to the divine presence in the womb of Mary and therefore as the means for divinization. Also, using Moses as an example, he claims that just as God in his mercy limited himself by coming to Moses, he does the same for feeble human beings. In his <u>Hymn on Epiphany</u>, No. 8, he explains:

God in His mercy stooped and came down,
to mingle His compassion with the water,
and to blend the nature of His majesty
with the wretched bodies of men.
He made occasion by the water
to come down and to dwell in us;
like to the occasion of mercy
when He came down and dwelt in the womb:
O the mercies of God
Who seeks for Himself all occasions to dwell in us!

To the cave in Horeb He stooped and came down,
and on Moses He caused His majesty to dwell;
He imparted His glorious splendor to mortals.
There was therein a figure of Baptism:

103

He Who came down and dwelt in it,
tempers within the water
the might of His majesty,
that He may dwell in the feeble
On Moses dwelt the Breath,
and on you the Perfecting of Christ.

That might then none could endure;
not Moses chief of deliverers,
nor Elijah chief of zealots;
and the Seraphim too veil their faces,
for it is the might that subdues all.
His mercy mingled gentleness
in the water and by the oil;
that mankind in its weakness
might be able to stand before Him
when covered by the water and the oil.[8]

In his Hymn on the Ephiphany, No. 9, Ephrem further teaches that Baptism renders humans children of the Spirit and that Christ becomes the new Adam and the new head of the Body of Christians. Ephrem also symbolizes the power of divinization by speaking of a column extending from the Jordan to the heavens. He describes John as seeing the Spirit on the head of Christ who as the "Head of the Highest" was baptized and became "Head on earth". Christians are therefore children of the Spirit, members of Christ who is the Head. Ephrem continues:

...Open wide your minds and see, my brethren,
the secret column in the air,
whose base is fixed from the midst of the water
unto the door of the Highest Place,
like the ladder that Jacob saw.
Lo! by it came down the light unto Baptism,
and by it the soul goes up to Heaven,
that in one love we may be mingled.[9]

In regard to this citation, it can also be noted that in the earlier Syriac tradition, Christ was seen as consecrating the waters of the Jordan in terms of the imagery of fire. This may be a reflection of Isaiah 6, 6. S. Brock cites James of Serug as saying: "The Holy One came to the water to go down to be baptized; his fire kindled among the waters and set them alight." The Jordan was sometimes referred to as a furnace.[10]

The Maronite liturgy in the ritual for Baptism

reflects the tradition. It says concerning Christ:
"...He who was without need or lacking was baptized in
the Jordan consecrating for us this womb which is the
baptismal font, a salutary and fruitful womb. He,
thence, according to his design, yours and that of the
Holy Spirit, lived in the world, in three dwellings:
the womb of flesh, the baptismal womb, and the obscure
dwellings of sheol..."[11]

## The Spirit on the waters

One with Christ in divinizing the waters of the
Jordan is the action of his Spirit. The same Spirit
who descends on Mary to bring about Christ in her womb,
exercises a similar action in the waters of Jordan,
which becomes the maternal womb of all Christians.[12]
In his **Hymn on the Epiphany, No. 6,** Ephrem speaks of
the Spirit descending and consecrating the waters "by
his brooding". At the Jordan the Spirit descended only
on Christ, but now he descends and takes his abode on
all who are baptized.[13]  In his **Sermon on the Lord, No.
53,** Ephrem understands the Spirit as now present in the
waters of Baptism itself:

> Therefore, because the Spirit was with the Son,
> he came to John to receive from him baptism,
> that he might mingle with the visible waters
> the invisible Spirit; that they whose bodies
> should feel the moistening of the water, their
> souls should feel the gift of the Spirit; that
> even as the bodies outwardly feel the pouring
> of the water upon them, so the souls inwardly
> may feel the pouring of the Spirit upon them.[14]

## All waters consecrated by Christ

The entry of Christ into the Jordan was understood as consecrating all waters of the earth.  S.
Brock cites James of Serug saying: "...the entire nature of the waters percieved that you had visited them
-- seas, deeps, rivers, springs and pools all thronged
together to receive the blessing from your footsteps."[15]

S. Brock uses this belief to explain why in some
Antiochene baptismal rituals the 'epiklesis' is referred
to Christ rather than the Father. He reasons that if
the tradition was that Christ sanctified all baptismal
water, then it is understandable that he should be
asked to send his Spirit to bring about sanctification.[16]

105

## The Effects of Baptism

### Baptism as a 'new womb'

Symbolizing and effecting redemption, Baptism reverses the effects of Adam's sin and begins to restore the original condition. Most importantly, baptism is seen as a new creation and new birth. The water of baptism easily represents the idea of a womb, and is also seen as symbolizing primeval water. Ephrem develops this idea in his Hymn on the Epiphany, No. 13, when he says: "Baptism is a mother who engenders each day spiritual infants and gives to God new and holy sons." [17]

Ephrem ties in the idea of new birth with forgiveness of sins. In his Hymn on Virginity, No. 7, he speaks of the baptized being anointed with oil and receiving forgiveness from all their sins. The baptized who were sordid with sin arise from the "second womb" of baptism, pure as infants. [18]

James of Serug refers to a new birth given to Adam, and relates baptism to immortality and spirituality. He says:

A new mother instead of the old has been given to the prostrate Adam; and when she gives birth to him he will find salvation.
For instead of Eve, Baptism has entered and taken her stand
ready to give birth to immortality in spirituality;
instead of that mother who gave birth to feeble corpses,
this mother gives birth to living beings, rational and immortal...
The womb of water, in place of the bodily womb has begun to produce rational 'images', in a spiritual way. [19]

This theme is reflected in the Baptismal rituals. As early as a Baptismal ritual attributed to Timothy of Alexandria (+477) we find the following prayer:

Blessed art thou, O Lord our God, through whose great and unutterable gift the baptismal water has been sanctified by the coming of thy living and holy Spirit, so as to become the spiritual

womb which gives birth to the new man in place
of the old..."[20]

The Maronite liturgy reflects clearly and pre-
cisely this idea of Baptism as a new womb. In the Baptismal ritual the prayer over the water declares: "As
the womb of our mother Eve gave birth to mortal children subject to corruption, let this Baptism become a
womb which will give birth to spiritual and immortal
children. As the Holy Spirit hovered over the waters
at the creation and gave life to animals of every kind,
let Him hover over this Baptism, dwell within it and
sanctify it. Let it change the earthly Adam into a
spiritual one. Let all who enter into it receive
spiritual strength in place of the weakness of the
flesh. Toghether with this natural life let them receive a spiritual one, and in addition to this visible
world, let them receive a participation in the invisible one, and in place of a weak spirit, let your
life-giving Spirit dwell within them."

A similar theology is reflected in the "sedro"
prayer of the Maronite Morning Office of the First Sunday after Epiphany. It prays: "O God who in your love
have become human, you were born corporeally to allow
humans to accede to filial adoption and you have made
them children of your Father by water and the Spirit.
You, who formed children in the womb, have voluntarily
enclosed yourself in the womb to renew the image of
Adam that the corruption of sin had tarnished and de-
graded, and you have renewed it by the fire of the pure
spiritual light that is baptism. You, who have no
need, have come to be baptized to sanctify the waters
of the Jordan in your goodness. ...as in your baptism
you have vested us in the adornement of glory and
marked us with the seal of your living and Holy Spirit,
so you have called us to be spiritual children by the
second birth, that of baptism which purifies sins.
Likewise, by your powerful and invicible force, make us
glorify you with smiling faces, confident as very loved
children..."

A new 'Image'

As we have seen, a key element in Syriac anthropology is that humans are in the image of God, an image
first stamped on Adam, but distorted when Adam sinned.
Baptism is seen as restoring this image. For example,
in his Hymn on Virginity, No. 7, Ephrem chants:

The royal image is painted with visible colors.
With visible oil is painted the hidden image of
the invisible king.  Baptism has conceived in
its womb those who are signed.  It creates a
new image in place of the image corrupted by
the first Adam.[21]

In his Hymn on Virginity, No. 48, Ephrem sees in the
restored image a sign of divinization: "The son has
made beautiful the servant's deformity and he has become a god, just as he desired."[22]

James of Serug continues the tradition and
stresses that the new human is cast in the imprint of
Christ himself.  He presents Christ explaining to John
the Baptiser:

I am entering the furnace of water
so that mankind, who have grown worn out, may
be recast with my imprint
I desire them to come, as I do, to the fountain
so that they may be imprinted spiritually with
my coin.[23]

The Maronite liturgy reflects this teaching.  In
a Baptismal ritual attributed to James of Serug, the
priest imposing incense recites the following prayer:

O God who, by your love, have become man, being
born of the holy Virgin in an incomprehensible
fashion without human seed, to lead men to the
condition of sons of your Father, making them
sons of your Father by means of water; you who
fashion children in the womb, have freely become a child to renew the image of Adam damaged
and having grown old by sin, renewing him by
the fire of that spiritual and salutary Furnace, which is the baptismal font.[24]

'Robe of Glory'

Besides divine filiation and the restoration of
the divine image, the 'robe of glory', as we have seen,
symbolizes sanctification.  If Adam and Eve lost the
robe of glory,  Christ brings it back, and it is restored in Baptism.  Ephrem in his Hymn on the Epiphany,
No. 12 teaches:

In Baptism Adam found again

that glory that was among the trees of Eden
He went down, and received it out of the water;
he put it on, and went up and was adorned
therein.
Blessed be He that has mercy on all.

...the wedded pair were adorned in Eden;
but the serpent stole their crowns:
yet mercy crushed down the accursed one,
and made the wedded pair goodly in their raiment.
Blessed be he that has mercy on all! [25]

James of Serug repeats this theme when he says:
"Baptism gives back to Adam the robe of glory which the
serpent had stolen from among the trees." For him,
besides the robe, the baptized also put on "zayna",
protective armor against the arrows of Satan.[26]

In his Hymn on the Epiphany, No. 4, Ephrem reflects on the idea of the baptized putting off their
garments, and putting on Christ. In so doing, he also
brings in the ideas of deification and immortality. He
says:

Descend my sealed brothers, put on your Lord,
and be rejoined to his lineage, for He is son
of a great lineage,
as He said in His Word.

From on high is his Nature, and from beneath
his Vesture,
Each that puts off his vesture, commingled is
that vesture, with His Vesture forever.

You too in the water, receive from him the vesture,
that wastes not or is lost for it is the vesture that vests
them that are vested in it forever.[27]

The Maronite ritual of Baptism in its "sedro"
prays: "...as you clothed us with the robe of glory and
signed us with the seal of the living Holy Spirit, and
as you called us to become spiritual children reborn
through Baptism, make us worthy to glorify..."

## The Gift of the Spirit

If Baptism brings about rebirth, its second

great gift is that of the Spirit. The Spirit not only consecrates the waters, but also resides in the new Christian. Aphraat who, as we have seen, bases his anthropology on a distinction of body, soul, and spirit, focuses on the reception of the Holy Spirit in Baptism as essential to humanity's future immortality. In his Demonstration, No 4 on Monks, he teaches that at Baptism when the priests invoke the Holy Spirit, the heavens open and the Spirit descends upon the waters. The baptized are clothed with the Spirit, who is distant from those born of the flesh, until they are baptized. In the first birth, humans are created with animal souls, but in baptism they receive the Holy Spirit and are not again subject to death. When humans die, the animal soul is buried with the body, but the heavenly spirit goes to Christ. Aphraat continues: "And the animal spirit shall be swallowed up in the heavenly Spirit, and the whole man shall become spiritual, since his body is possessed by it <the Spirit>. And death shall be swallowed up in life, and body shall be swallowed up in Spirit." [28]

In His Hymn on the Epiphany, No. 5, Ephrem describes the presence of the Spirit:

Descend, my brothers, put on from the waters of Baptism the Holy Spirit;
be joined with the spirits that minister to the Godhead.
For lo! He is the fire that secretly, seals also his flock,
by the Three Spiritual Names, wherein the Evil One is put to flight. [29]

James of Serug reflecting on the biblical teaching declares that through the Spirit, Christ has made us his brothers and sisters. The Father sends the Spirit of his Son into our hearts, and through the Spirit we can truly call God 'our Father'. [30]

The Maronite ritual for Baptism attributed to James of Serug prays in the blessing of the water: "...Let all who enter into it receive spiritual strength in place of the weakness of the flesh. Together with this natural life let them receive a spiritual one, and in addition to this visible world, let them receive a participation in the invisible one, and in place of a weak spirit let your life giving Spirit dwell within them."

110

## Other Effects

Based on the Scriptures, a principal effect of Baptism is the forgiveness of sin. This is repeated often by the Syriac fathers. One way in which the removal of sins is described is under the idea of regaining of freedom. In the <u>Hymn on the Epiphany, No. 4</u>, Ephrem uses the imagery of leaven in the waters to describe the freedom Christ effects:

...The Godhead in the water, lo! has mingled
His leaven;
for the creatures of dust, that leaven raises
up,
and the Godhead joins them.

For it is the leaven of the Lord, that can
glide into the bondman,
and raise him to freedom; it has joined the
bondman to the lineage
of Him the Lord of all.

For the bondman who has put on Him, Who makes
all free in the waters,
though bondman he be on earth, is son of the
free on high,
for freedom he has put on.[31]

Philoxenus of Mabboug sees in the baptism of Christ a "type of the consummation of the world in that when he was baptized Jesus fulfilled His Father's will, and created all things new both visible and invisible.[32] For Ephrem baptism is both a recalling of the state of humans before the sin in Paradise and a pledge of the world to come. Being joined to the Church by Baptism, humans are in route to the future kingdom.[33]

The Maronite liturgy summarizes the effects of Baptism in the "sedro" of the Sunday after Epiphany: "O God, You became man out of your love for us. You were born of the flesh to gather humanity to the adoption of Your Father to make them his children through water and the Holy Spirit. O creator of Life, You became a man in order to renew the image of Adam, which grew old and distorted because of sin....You have clothed us with Your baptism, the robe of glory and the seal of the Holy Spirit. You have called us to be spiritual children through the second birth of baptism, which purifies all sinners..."

111

# The Cross and Baptism

If the Baptism of Christ in the Jordan origi-
nates the mystery of Baptism, it is also a foreshadowing of Christ's death on the Cross and the blood
and water that will pour forth from his pierced side.
For the Syriac fathers, the water from the side of
Christ could only be living water, and therefore another element in the constitution of the mystery of
Baptism. In his <u>Hymn on Baptism, No. 11</u>, Ephrem declares: "Baptism is the well-spring of life, which the
Son of God opened by his Life; and from his side it has
brought forth streams."[34] A similar theme is developed
in his <u>Hymn on Epiphany, No. 5</u>, when he says: "Lo! from
the side of Christ flowed the stream that bestowed
life. The Gentiles drank that were weary, and in it
forgot their pains."[35]

Ephrem further develops the idea of the Cross as
a Cross of light with its relationship with the waters
of Baptism. In his <u>Hymn on the Epiphany, No. 13</u>, he
says:

> The Crucified is a brilliant sun who diffused
> his light in the water <of baptism>. He calls
> the nations who are held in darkness to descend
> <in the water>, to be clothed in the light, to
> adorn themselves, and give out rays in his
> light.[36]

As also noted previously, James of Serug speaks
more explicitly of Baptism being established on the
Cross. He sees the new birth occurring in water and
blood, and that the Holy Spirit is breathed into the
newly baptized. In his homily on the three baptisms,
James says:

> Christ came and opened up baptism by his Cross,
> so that it should be a mother of life for the
> world in place of Eve
> water and blood for the fashioning of spiritual
> babes
> flowed forth from it, and baptism became the
> mother of life.
> No previous baptism <<u>i.e.</u> of Moses or of John>
> ever gave the Holy Spirit
> only the baptism which was opened by the Son of
> God on the Cross;
> it gives birth to children spiritually with
> 'the water and the blood',

112

and, instead of a soul, the Holy Spirit is breathed into them. [37]

This belief is reflected in the Maronite Baptismal liturgy. In the ancient ritual, the 'epiklesis' prayer includes the following: "...Let the Holy Spirit descend upon this water and sanctify it. Let Him fill it with unfailing strength, let Him bless it. Let it become as the water that flowed from the side of Your only Son upon the cross, so that it may purify and cleanse all who are baptized in it. May it clothe each one with the robe of heavenly justice and with the armor of faith against the attacks of the evil one." [38]

Along these lines, A. Mouhanna concludes from his work on the Maronite Baptismal liturgy that the proper day for the celebration of Baptism in the Maronite Church is Epiphany, not Easter. He cites the medieval Maronite canonical work <u>Kitab al-Hoda</u> as an indication. It says: "...He <Jesus> was baptized by John, his servant; when he received the Holy Spirit and baptism, he fasted for forty days and forty nights, to teach us by that that every Christian ought first to be baptized and receive the spiritual vestment of consecrated water. And, when he puts on the Holy Spirit by baptism, he ought then to practice the first of all obligations: the fast of forty days, as the Savior of the world had done." (See: P. Fahed, <u>Kitab al-Huda</u>, Aleppo, 1935, p. 113) [39]

## Anointings

Besides the waters of Baptism, an integral element in the process of initiation into the flock of Christ is the action of anointing. We will discuss below the question of the pre- and post-baptismal anointing in the Syriac Church. When one considers, as we have already seen, the symbolism of olive oil and the vine and even the 'tree of life' in the Syriac mind, it is not surprising that anointing should be the vehicle of representing both the presence of Christ and also the action of the Spirit.

Since the title Christ itself means the "Anointed One", Ephrem in several places speaks of chrism as representing Christ. In his <u>Hymn on the Epiphany, No. 3</u>, he explains:

Chirst and chrism are conjoined; the secret with the visible is mingled: the chrism anoints

113

visibly; Christ seals secretly, the lambs new-
born and spiritual, the prize of His twofold
victory; for He engendered it of the chrism,
and He gave it birth of the water.

How exalted are your Orders! For she that
was a sinner anointed, as a handmaid, the feet
of her Lord. But for you, as though His minister, Christ by the hand of His servants, seals
and anoints your bodies. It befits Him the
Lord of the flock, that in His own person He
seal His sheep.[40]

In the Hymn on the Faith, No. 82, Ephrem refers
to the baptized as divers seeking the pearl and also
takes the occasion to describe the soul being saved
from evil. He says:

In symbol and truth Leviathan is trodden down
by mortals: the baptized, like divers, strip
and put on oil, as a symbol of Christ
they snatched you and came up: stripped,
they seized the soul from his embittered mouth.[41]

S. Brock points out that in a number of hymns "On Oil
and the Olive" Ephrem further deals with the theme of
oil as a type of Christ <the "Anointed One">[42]

The fact that chrism continued to represent
Christ in the Syriac tradition is seen in such writings
as those of Jacob of Edessa. In his "Discourse on the
Myron", he explains:

Thus, by means of a comparison with what cannot
be compared, it portrays for us Jesus, the
simple one who came to composition <"rukkaba">,
<Jesus> who is the overflowing fountainhead of
divine fragrance, filling the intellect with
divine assignments, as a result of the wonderful quality of the scent of knowledge.[43]

If the oil represents Christ, "the Anointed", it
is the Holy Spirit who anointed Christ at his Baptism.
Therefore, oil is the vehicle whereby the Holy Spirit
effects his power. Ephrem in his Hymn on Virginity,
No. 7 teaches this clearly, as well as the idea of the
anointing as a sealing. He says:

The oil is the dear friend of the Holy Spirit,

114

it serves Him, following Him like a disciple. With it the Spirit signs priests and anoints kings; for with the oil the Holy Spirit imprints His work on His sheep. Like a signet ring whose impression is left on wax, so the hidden seal of the Spirit is imprinted by oil on the bodies of those who are anointed in Baptism; thus are they marked in the baptismal mystery.[44]

Theodore of Mopsuestia echoes this tradition in his fourteenth homily. He teaches that at the Baptism in the Jordan, when the Holy Spirit descended on Chirst like a dove, He was anointed. This is what Christ is referring to in Luke 4, 18, when he says that 'The Spirit of the Lord is upon me'. Also, Acts 10, 38 speaks of 'Jesus of Nazareth, whom God has anointed with the holy spirit and with power.' Theodore concludes that these texts show that the Holy Spirit is never separated from Christ, and that the same is true of those who have been anointed with oil. The anointing has a durable effect and is not separated from them. Theodore declares: "Therefore, it is right that you also should receive the signing on your forehead".[45] T. Curtain claims that John Chrysostom and Theodore of Mopsuestia associate the gift of the Spirit, not with anointing, but with the imposition of hands and consignation. But, the majority of Eastern writiers associate the gift of the Spirit with anointing. These include Cyril of Jerusalem, Gregory Nazienzus, Cyril of Alexandria, Theodoret of Cyrus, Narsai, and Pseudo-Dionysius.[46]

We should also keep in mind that while Ephrem and the other Syriac writers focus their attention on Christ or the Spirit, there are a number of references to the indwelling of the Trinity. For example, in his Hymn on the Epiphany, No. 3, Ephrem states: "...The Spirit dwelt in him <David> and made song in him. Your anointing which you have is greater, our Father and Son and Holy Spirit have moved and come down to dwell in you."[47]

## Seal and Protection

As we have seen, the idea of 'seal' has a rich history in the Jewish and Syriac traditions. It has the meaning of ownership, mark of authenticity, and takes on an eschatological character. In the Jewish tradition it also referred to circumcision. In the

Syriac world it took on these meanings, as well as the idea of protection in combat against evil. This concept of protection is especially related to being signed on the forehead.[48]

Ephrem sees the gesture of sealing as distinguishing the true flock, and in so doing serves as a protection from sin and evil. In the Hymn on the Epiphany, No. 3, he declares:

> ...But you are the flock, among the profane and unbelievers, and the Truth by the chrism is your seal, to separate you from the strayed.
> ...The chrism of Christ separates the sons of the mystery from strangers: and by it they that are within are separated, and known from them that are without.
> ...The sheep of Christ leaped for joy, to receive the seal of life, that ensign of kings which has ever put sin to flight. The wicked one by the ensign is routed, iniquities by thy sign are scattered. Come, you sheep, receive your seal, which puts to flight them that devour you![49]

For James of Serug, "Baptism, the daughter of lights, provides the mark of the king." James speaks of the mark both in the image of the branding of sheep, and also in terms of coins being stamped.[50]

Jacob of Edessa continues the tradition when he says:

> This oil, then, is the beginning of the heavenly path, the ladder that leads up to heaven, the armor against hostile powers, the indissoluble imprint of the king, the sign which delivers from the fire, the guardian of the faithful, driving off the demons; it gives joy to angels, it is both living and life-giving, full of great things entrusted of wonderous mysteries.[51]

In the ancient Maronite Baptismal ritual, the "sedro" prayer petitions: "...And may all harms of the enemy be far removed from their lives, and may they have only thy holy seal as a guide and guardian..."[52]

116

Ephrem in his Hymn on Virginity, No. 7 declares clearly that oil purifies and forgives sin. He describes oil as a "beneficial fountain" that wipes out the sins as the flood had destroyed the unclean. The oil removes sins in Baptism, because sin is drowned in the water. The oil like Christ out of love pays for debts not its own.[53]

Jacob of Edessa in his "Discourse on the Myron" speaks of several meanings and effects of chrism. For example, referring to the Old Testament practice of anointing prophets, priests, and kings, he explains that Christians are anointed and thereby perfected as priests and disciples of the Apostles. Therefore, they stand before God "as a holy people, a redeemed assembly, a royal priesthood, a choice and sweet-scented nation, and one resplendent in an invisible garment.["][54] Continuing, he uses the bridal imagery of the Old Testament and states that the Church as bride of God the Word who became man "compares him to oil because he anointed and united with his eternal Godhead our temporal humanity."[55]

### Pre- and Post-Baptismal Anointing

The consensus among scholars seems to be that in the early Syriac tradition, the principal anointing representing the action of the Holy Spirit occurred before baptismal immersion. S. Brock and others have observed that the Pauline teaching on baptism as a burial and rising with Christ is not found in early Syriac baptismal texts. In fact, Brock points out that the pre-baptismal anointing is 'charismatic' in character as compared to the 'cathartic and exorcistic' role that this anointing has in other traditions.[56] Leonell Mitchell claims from a study of the works of Ephrem that the liturgy of Baptism consists principally of a pre-baptismal anointing and baptismal immersion. He notes that in the Hymn on the Epiphany, No. 3, Ephrem speaks of the sealing with oil of lepers at their cleansing, before the priest leads them to the washing.[57] Gabrielle Winkler notes that the oldest Syriac sources of the third and fourth centuries regularly call the pre-baptismal anointing of the head "rushma" (sign, mark), while the term "hatma" (seal) is normally reserved for the post-baptismal anointing that was introduced at the end of the fourth century.[58] S. Brock adds that the pre-baptismal anointing was originally on the forehead, but later it was extended to

117

the whole body, which sometimes gave rise to two separate pre-baptismal anointings.[59]

On the other hand, from the fifth century on there are references to a post-baptismal anointing. A possible reference to it is found in Theodore of Mopsuestia. It is witnessed to by the Apostolic Constitutions, Pseudo-Dionysius, Severus and John of Tella.[60]

Several factors may have been involved in the institution of a post-baptismal anointing. G. Winkler and S. Brock observe that by the end of the fourth century a stress is given to the Pauline understanding of Baptism as a death and burial. The font comes to be seen as a grave rather than a womb, and the pre-baptismal anointing loses its charismatic character. Therefore, the change of emphasis from a Johannine to a Pauline imagery resulted in the reinterpretation of the pre-baptismal anointing as something cathartic and protective.[61]

E.C. Ratcliff stresses that the Church of Jerusalem and perhaps its proximity to the holy places might have accounted for the emphasis on the death and burial of Christ. Cyril of Jerusalem describes two distinct anointings. In the third mystagogical homily he speaks of a pre-baptismal anointing which was made with oil of exorcism, and in the fourth homily of an anointing with chrism ("myron"). Cyril explains that the new ceremony of anointing with "myron" is a symbol of the coming of the Holy Spirit upon Jesus to 'anoint' him after his ascent out of the water from his baptism. Therefore, the focus is now on the Holy Spirit descending on Christ after he ascended from the Jordan. Differing from his predecessors, Cyril distinguishes between Chirst's descent into the water and the event which followed it. Cyril reinterprets the first anointing as the means of "expelling every trace of the adversary and purify the traces of sin." For Cyril, following the Pauline idea of Romans 6, 3-5, the three-fold submersion in the water now symbolizes Christ's three days of burial in the tomb.[62]

While rejecting Ratcliff's topographical argument regarding Jerusalem and the holy places, G. Winkler also cites especially the writings of Cyril of Jerusalem, along with those of John Chrysostom and Theodore of Mopsuestia, as focusing on the soul's confrontation with demonic powers, rather than stressing the charismatic effect of the anointing. The preparation of the catechumens for Baptism is viewed as a battle with Satan. She points out that catechumens underwent daily excorcisms during their period of preparation, and that this became a predominant factor in the western half of Syria and Palestine.[63] Winkler reasons that since the preparatory rites now had a predominantly cathartic and excorcistic character and were seen as an indispensible condition for receiving the Spirit, the pre-baptismal anointing could no longer be the actual gift of the Spirit. A catechumen had to be purified and have his sins washed away before he could receive the Spirit. Winkler claims that an anointing after baptism was introduced to signify the coming of the Spirit.[64]

S. Brock is of the opinion that the shift in the meaning of the pre-baptismal anointing is due to a shift in emphasis that occurred with the rapid Christianization of the Roman Empire in the fourth century after Constantine's conversion. Prior to this time its Jewish origins had a strong influence on Syriac Christianity. After this time, a more hellenized character manifested itself. In the early period, the pre-baptismal anointing was the new Christian equivalent of circumcision, and the baptised were understood as anointed into the royal priesthood. Therefore the "rushma" signified ownership, sonship, and priesthood. According to Brock, the new mentality encouraged a protective interpretation of the anointing. He claims that since the Old Testament basis for the anointing as signifying the anointing of priests had a charismatic character, this would also tend to be pushed in the background as Christiantiy became more institutionalized. There is now more attention paid to the baptism of Christ as the model for Christian baptism, and also to the fact that the Holy Spirit only appeared after Christ had gone up from the water. As we have noted above, more emphasis is given to the Pauline interpretation of Christ's baptism signifying death and resurrection. For Brock, the imagery of the font as a grave clashes with the earlier understanding of the "rushma" as signifying anything positive such as sonship. Therefore, the way is open for the introduction of a post-baptismal anointing to incorporate these positive elements. Brock concludes that the tensions brought about by the developments of the late fourth century "created an inner dynamic within the rite itself that cried out for the introduction of a new post-baptismal anointing to take over those characteristics

119

which it was no longer thought possible to associate with the rushma." The rushma was left with only a protective and cathartic meaning.[65]

Another possible element affecting the institution of a post-baptismal anointing was perhaps the decision of the Council of Laodicaea (363) on what to do with those who were validly baptized by heretics but did not receive the gift of the Holy Spirit. The Council teaches that those who have been validly baptized but were heretical at the time should anathematize the heresy, learn the Creed, and then, after having been anointed with holy chrism, communicate in the holy mysteries. This understanding would seem to impose a post-baptismal anointing in order to receive the Spirit, for those already baptized.[66]

B. Botte and others conjecture that this anointing to receive the "gift of the Spirit" is then extended to all. This would explain the forty-eighth canon of the Council of Laodicaea which stated: "It is necessary that those who have been baptized be, after baptism, anointed with celestial chrism and rendered participants of the kingdom of Christ."[67] G. Winkler is also skeptical about this explanation of post-baptismal anointing, and tends to believe that the inner dynamic at play in changing the meaning of Baptism from the memory of Christ's baptism in the Jordan to a cathartic emphasis is the best explanation.[68]

We might conclude the discussion with a caution made by S. Brock and others. The baptismal rite in the Syriac Church always had two constitutive elements, anointing and baptism, irrespective of the order in which these elements occur. However, the development of the post-baptismal anointing both as to place and meaning was quite different from the mentality of the West. Therefore, it would be misleading to try to draw parallels between the two traditions.[69]

# Notes to Chapter Nine

1. P. Verghese, "The relation between Baptism, 'Confirmation', and the Eucharist in the Syrian Orthodox Church," Studia Liturgica, vol. 4 (1965) p. 84.

2. R. Murray, Symbols of Church and Kingdom, p. 21.

3. Verghese, art. cit, pp. 82-3.

4. W. de Vries, "Théologie des Sacraments chez les Syriens monophysites," L'Orient Syrien, vol. 8 (1963) pp. 264-5.

5. L. Mitchell, "Four Fathers on Baptism: St. John Chrysostom, St. Ephrem, Theodore of Mopsuestia, Narsai," Studies in the Syrian Baptismal Rites, ed. by Jacob Vellian, p. 53.

6. J. Lecuyer, "La théologie de l'anaphore selon les pères de l'école d'Antioche," L'Orient Syrien, vol. 6 (1961) pp. 389-96.

7. S. Brock, "The Syrian Baptismal Rites," Concilium, vol. 122 (1979) p. 99.

8. Nicene and Post-Nicene Fathers, p. 276.

9. Ibid., p. 279.

10. S. Brock, "Baptismal themes in the writings of Jacob of Serugh," Orientalia Christiana Analecta, vol. 205 (1978) p. 327.

11. A. Mouhanna, Les Rites de l'Initiation dans l'Église Maronite (Rome: Pontificium Institutum Orientalium Studorum, 1978) pp. 50-1.

12. G. Saber, La Théologie Baptismale de Saint Ephrem, p. 172.

13. Nicene and Post-Nicene Fathers, p. 273.

14. Mitchell, art. cit., p. 47.

15. Brock, "Baptismal themes...", p. 327.

16. Brock, "The Epiklesis in the Antiochene Baptismal Ordines," _Orientalia Christiana Analecta,_ vol. 197, p. 197.

17. Cited by Saber, _op. cit._, p. 177.

18. S. Brock, _The Harp of the Spirit,_ p. 50.

19. Brock, "Baptismal themes...", pp. 345-6.

20. Brock, "A New Syrian Ordo attributed to Timothy of Alexandria," _Studies on the Syrian Baptismal Rites,_ p. 82.

21. Cited by Saber, _op. cit._, p. 162.

22. Brock, "Syrian Baptismal rites...", p. 103.

23. Brock, "Baptismal themes...", pp. 337-8.

24. Mouhanna, _op. cit._, pp. 16-7.

25. _Nicene and Post-Nicene Fathers,_ p. 282.

26. Brock, "Baptismal themes...", pp. 336-7.

27. _Nicene and Post-Nicene Fathers,_ p. 271.

28. _Ibid._, pp. 371 ff.

29. _Ibid._, p. 272.

30. Brock, "Baptismal themes...", p. 335.

31. _Nicene and Post-Nicene Fathers,_ p. 271.

32. Douglas J. Fox, _The "Matthew-Luke Commentary" of Philoxenus,_ p. 253.

33. Saber, _op. cit._, pp. 173-4.

34. Mitchell, _art. cit._, p. 46.

35. _Nicene and Pos-Nicene Fathers,_ p. 273.

36. Cited by Saber, _op. cit._, p. 178.

37. Cited by Brock, "The Epiklesis...", p. 212.

38. See: Brock, "A New Syrian Ordo..." p. 81, and S.

Brock, "A Short Melkite Baptismal Service in Syriac,"
*Parole de l'Orient*, vol. 3 (1972) p. 124.

39. Cited by Mouhanna, *op. cit.*, p. 260.

40. *Nicene and Post-Nicene Fathers*, p. 269.

41. Brock, *op. cit*, p. 33.

42. *Ibid.*, p. 47.

43. S. Brock, "Jacob of Edessa's Discoure on the Myron," *Oriens Christianus*, vol. 63 (1979) p. 33.

44. Brock, *op. cit.*, p. 50.

45. T. Curtain, *The Baptismal Liturgy of Theodore of Mopsuestia* (Washington, D.C.: Catholic University of America Press, 1970) pp. 339-40.

46. *Ibid.*, pp. 358-9.

47. *Nicene and Post-Nicene Fathers*, p. 270.

48. V. Van Vossel, "Le terme et la notion de 'sceau' chez les Syriens Orientaux," *L'Orient Syrien*, vol. 10 (1965) pp. 244-56. See also: A.F.J. Kiljn, "Baptism in the Acts of Thomas," *Studies on the Syrian Baptismal Rites*, p. 61.

49. *Nicene and Post-Nicene Fathers*, p. 269-71.

50. Brock, "Baptismal themes...", p. 338.

51. Brock, "Jacob of Edessa's...", p. 33.

52. Brock, "A New Syrian...", p. 74.

53. Brock, *op. cit.*, p. 50.

54. Brock, "Jacob of Edessa's...", p. 30.

55. *Ibid.*, p. 31.

56. Brock, "Syrian Baptismal...", p. 100.

57. Mitchell, *art. cit.*, p. 44.

58. G. Winkler, "The Orignial Meaning of the Pre-Baptismal Anointing and its Implications," *Worship*,

vol. 52 (1978) p. 27.

59. Brock, "Syrian Baptismal...", p. 98. See also: S. Brock, "The Transition to a Post-Baptismal Anointing in the Antiochene Rite," The Sacrifice of Praise, ed. by Bryan D. Spinks (Rome: Edizioni Liturgiche, 1981) p. 215.

60. A. Raes, "Où se trouve la confirmation dans le rite Syro-Oriental," L'Orient Syrien, vol. 1 (1956) pp. 244-5. See also: Brock, "A Short Melkite...", pp. 120-1.

61. Brock, "The Syrian...", p. 100; and "The Epiklesis...", p. 207.

62. E.C. Ratcliff, "The Old Syrian Baptismal Tradition and its Resttlement under the Influence of Jerusalem in the Fourth Century," Studies on the Syrian Baptismal Rites, pp. 88-98.

63. Winkler, art. cit., pp. 39-40.

64. Ibid., p. 40-1.

65. Brock, "The Transition...", pp. 217-25.

66. B. Botte, "Post-Baptismal Anointing in the Ancient Patriarchate of Antioch," Studies on the Syrian Baptismal Rites, pp. 63-71.

67. Raes, art. cit., pp. 245-6.

68. Winkler, art. cit., p. 42, note 63.

69. Brock, "The Syrian Baptismal...", pp. 98-9.

# CHAPTER TEN

CHRISTIAN INITIATION, Part 2

The Eucharist

From the earliest tradition the Eucharist was seen as the completion of initiation into the discipleship of Christ. It is the Eucharist which constitutes Church and which is the central mystery. All other sacramental celebrations receive their meaning from the Eucharist. One could use a reverse form of reasoning and claim that the purpose of Baptism itself is to render one worthy of partaking of the Eucharist. All these themes are to be found among the Syriac fathers.

In the eastern mind, one does not give priority to the idea of Church as sacrament, and then understand the seven sacraments by some form of analogy. Rather, it is Eucharist which is formative of the Church. Eucharist and Church are primordial realities, essentially bearing the same names: communion, body of Christ. The Eucharist imparts charity but within the conext of a visible fellowship. The other sacraments bring humans to a suitable state wherein they can participate fruitfully in the central sacrament. In this view, baptism is a preparation for eucharistic fellowship.[1]

As we have already seen, Ephrem considers the body of Christ as the vehicle of salvation. For him, that same body in which he healed humans and rose again, he gave us in sacramental form to heal us, to incorporate us in him in the Church, and to give us a pledge of his Resurrection.[2]

In another sense, as we have seen regarding revelation, the sacraments also represent a 'kenosis' of divine power in a creaturely reality. Ephrem in his Hymn on the Faith, No. 6 summarizes the kenosis involved in the sacraments, the Incarnation, and revelation:

> For in the Bread is eaten a strength not to be eaten
> and in the Wine is drunk a might not to be drunk;
> in the Oil we have anointing with a power not

for ointment to take pleasure and eat,
He has softened his appearance for the eyes and
his might in words, that the ear may hear him.[3]

From the earliest days of the Church, the Eucharist was seen as a great corporate act of the whole people. Theodore of Mopsuestia in his <u>Mystagogical Cathecheses</u> seems to pre-suppose that all who are present will partake of communion. He says:

The priest prays that the grace of the holy spirit may come also on all those present, in order that...they may be knit here as if into one body by the communion of the flesh of our Lord...[4]
...
All of us partake of it <the holy bread> equally, as all of us are one body of Christ our Lord, and all of us partake of the same body and blood. As through the second birth and through the holy spirit all of us become one body of Christ, so also by one nourishment of the holy sacrament, through which the grace of the holy spirit feeds us, all of us are in fellowship in Christ our Lord.

The Syriac writers presume a direct relationship between baptism and the Eucharist. If baptism incorporates the candidate into the Church, it also permits him to have access to the Holy Eucharist which is the cause and manifestation of that incorporation. For Aphraat: "When his heart has been circumcised from evil works, one then proceeds to baptism, the consummation of the true circumcision; he is joined to the people of God and participates in the body and blood of Christ." (<u>Demonstration No. 12 -- On the Passover</u>)[5] Ephrem draws a direct link between baptism and the eucharist when he declares: "Once this womb has given birth, the altar suckles and nurtures them: her children eat straight away, not milk, but perfect bread." (<u>Hymn on Virginity, No. 7</u>)[6] Ephrem also teaches the idea that Christian initiation involves incorporation in his <u>Hymn on the Epiphany, No. 3</u>:

The figure has passed, the truth is realized, with oil you have been signed, by baptism you have been rendered perfect, you have been mingled in the flock, you have been nourished with his body.

John Chrysostom gives the same witness in his Baptismal Instruction, No. 2 where he explains that when the newly baptized come from the font, they are led to the altar where they partake of the eucharist and become a dwelling place for the Holy Spirit. Also, the Apostolic Constitutions exhorts the assembly to pray that the candidates obtain forgiveness of sins by their admission and therefore be "worthy of the holy mysteries and of constant communion with the saints." The prayer reiterates that by their admission to the Church, they are partakers of the holy mysteries through the redemptive work of Christ. [7]

In the Syriac liturgical tradition we have a similar idea expressed in the blessing over the baptismal water which prays: "...And sanctify him in his soul and in his body and in his spirit. May he become a new child and a holy one, unto eternal life; and cause him to share in the holy body and blood, so that he may receive from them the propitiation of faults and forgiveness of sin, unto eternal life." [8]

## Eucharist as Mystery

The Syriac fathers were aware that in the Eucharist we are dealing with a great mystery, one that could be grasped only by faith. For Ephrem, as we have seen, the Eucharist is to be understood within the concept of image foreshadowing reality. In his Hymn on the Nativity, No. 11, he discusses the mystery of the Eucharist through a meditation by Mary:

For ⟨when⟩ I see that outward form of Yours before my eyes, the hidden Form is shadowed forth "in my mind," O holy One. In your visible form I see Adam, and in your hidden form I see Your Father, who is joined with you.

Have you then shown me alone Your Beauty in two Forms? Let Bread shadow forth you, and also the mind; dwell also in Bread and in the eaters thereof. In secret, and openly too, may Your Church see You, as well as Your Mother.
. . .
Lo! Your Image is shadowed forth in the blood of the grapes on the Bread; and it is shadowed forth on the heart with the finger of love, with the colors of faith. [9]

## Eucharist as Nourishment and Pledge of Immortality

Narsai in his twenty-first homily observes that after the neophyte is baptized, he is dressed in the white robe and receives the kiss of peace. Since he ought to begin his spiritual journey, he receives as appropriate nourishment the body and blood of the Lord.[10] As we have mentioned, Ephrem sees in the Incarnation not only God revealing himself to us in finite forms, but also the vehicle of our deification, ultimately by Christ giving his body to us. In his Homily on Our Lord, Ephrem explains that our deficiency is filled by the "leaven" from the body of Christ. While Christ does not literally cut off anything from his historical body, he gives us that which can be taken from him. Therefore, "of that which can be eaten, mortals eat him." Christ who possesses fullness and life in his body supplies for our deficiency and gives life to our mortality.[11]

In his Hymn on the Faith, No. 10, Ephrem declares in poetic form that the power of the Eucharist overcomes the power of death:

Your Bread kills the Devourer who had made us his bread,
Your Cup destroys death which was swallowing us up.
We have eaten you, Lord, we have drunk you,
not to exhaust you, but to live by you.[12]

The Maronite Office for Easter reflects this theme in the first "qolo". After speaking of the redemption of Christ, it observes: "...The Church contemplates his meal, immolated, become nourishment, and his blood ⟨become⟩ spiritual drink; and she savors it each day, until she shall rejoice with him in the kingdom of heaven.[13]

## Eucharist as Forgiving Sins

In the Syriac tradition as well as that of other Churches, the Eucharist is seen as forgiving sin. J.-M. Sauget has published a Syriac homily on the sinner attributed to a Bishop John which says:

Behold, it is written of the sinner that she kissed alone the feet of Christ, but it is not written that she received his body.
And if the kisses of the sinner, given with faith, shook and overthrew the fortress of

her debts, how much more we ourselves who em-
brace Him with love and receive Him with faith,
shall we be purified of our faults and sins,
and He will answer our requests.[14]

The Anaphora of the Twelve Apostles (and the
other anaphoras) declares in several places that the
Eucharist forgives sins. In the prayer after the epi-
kelesis it says: "May these holy life-giving mysteries
be for the pardon of faults, the forgiveness of sins,
the cure of our whole being and the strengthening of
our consciences so that none of your faithful perish."
In the prayer of abosultion it declares: "Make us
worthy to partake fully of these divine mysteries with
purity and sanctity that through them we may be for-
given as we forgive each other..."

The prayer of peace of the Anaphora of James
says: "...confident in your mercy and not in our wor-
thiness, we pray that this Mystery administered for the
salvation of your people will not be for our condemnation but for the forgiveness of our sins..."[15]
The prayer after the epiklesis in the Anaphora of Peter
petitions: "...so that these mysteries in which we
participate may purify our souls and bodies, forgive
our sins and grant us life..."

## Conclusion

The theology of the Syriac churches lays heavy
stress on the significance and interrelationship of the
sacraments of initiation. In baptism, one is dedicated
to the spirit, delivered from the impending judgment of
God, and incorporated into the company redeemed by
Christ's saving work. There is an illumination and
deification of the soul and a new birth of the body
with the putting on of Christ. Chrismation is the completion of baptism where the candidate is anointed with
the spirit as Christ was in the waters of the Jordan.
Both baptism and chrismation give one a foretaste of
future benefits and are a pledge of immortality. However, baptism and chrismation can be understood only
within the idea of church. They are administered and
received in the social context of Christ's body, the
church. On the other hand, it is the eucharist which
is formative of the church and imparts charity within
the context of a visible fellowhsip. Baptism and
chrismation are a preparation for Eucharistic fellowship and give the candidate the right to receive the
eucharist. The eucharist is the great corporate act of

all the people. As nourishment sustaining the new life received in baptism, the eucharist maintains the soul in its foretaste of immortal life. It is the chief instrument of divinization. The three sacraments initiate the candidate into the "mysteries" of the divine order. As matter informed by spirit, they manifest and symbolize in space and time, divine realites of a superior world.[16]

Notes to Chapter Ten

1. A. Hastings, "The Sacramentality of the Church," Eastern Churches Quarterly, vol. 16 (1964) pp. 222-225.

2. R. Murray, Symbols of Church and Kingdom, pp. 69-70.

3. Cited by R. Murray, "A Hymn of St. Ephrem to Christ on the Incarnation, the Holy Spirit, and the Sacraments," Eastern Churches Review, vol. 3 (1970-1) p. 147.

4. F. Reine, The Eucharistic Doctrine and Liturgy of the Mystagogical Catechesis of Theodore of Mopsuestia (Washington, D.C.: Catholic University Press, 1942) pp. 40, 48.

5. Cited by E. Duncan, Baptism in the Demonstrations of Aphraates the Persian Sage (Washington, D.C.: Catholic University Press, 1945) pp. 145 ff.

6. Cited by Brock, Harp of the Spirit, p. 50.

7. Cited by S. Beggiani, "Christian Initiation in the Eastern Churches," Living Light, vol. 11 (1974) pp. 542-3.

8. S. Brock, "A Short Melkite Baptismal Service in Syriac," Parole de l'Orient, vol. 3 (1972) p. 124.

9. Nicene and Post-Nicene Fathers, p. 245.

10. A. Raes, "Où se trouve la confirmation dans le rite syro-oriental?" L'Orient Syrien, vol. 1 (1956) p. 244.

11. Nicene and Post-Nicene Fathers, p. 310.

12. Murray, "A Hymn of St. Ephrem to Christ on the Incarnation...," p. 144.

13. E. Khalifé-Hachem, "Office Maronite du Grand Dimanche de la Résurrection: Texte du Ramso et Commentaire," Parole de l'Orient, vol. 6-7 (1975-6) pp. 288-9.

14. J.-M. Sauget, "Une Homélie Syriaque sur la pécheresse attribuée a un évêque Jean," Parole de l'Orient, vol. 6-7 (1975-6) p. 175.

15. See also: L. Ligier, "Dimension Personelle et Dimension Communitaire de la Pénitence en Orient," _La Maison Dieu_, vol. 90, pp. 173-5.

16. Beggiani, _art. cit._, p 546.

# CHAPTER ELEVEN

## ESCHATOLOGY

Eshcatology speculates on the fulfillment of God's plan of salvation. Christ's work is completed only when creation is restored to its original state. For individual Christians, the focus is primarily sacramental. Baptism and the Eucharist are the pledge of future fulfillment. The imagery for the future kingdom is basically biblical. In fact, while Syriac theology in general manifests a great tension and anticipation of the future world, it provides very little detail of the time to come.

According to Narsai, since God exists perpetually and is without beginning, He wished that the works that He made would remain without end. In this way, they are witnesses of His perpetuity. Through Christ, all shall be restored and accomplished. By Christ's mediation the will of the Hidden God will reign on all things and in all things, and there will be no fear of the truth. Christ shall return all things before the divine will, and shall invite the elect to heaven. Christ, the head of our life, has risen so that the visible body and the hidden soul will rise. By his resurrection, he has painted for us a figure of the day of our resurrection. Just as through Adam we have become mortal, so by the second Adam we have become immortal. The second Adam has made his way toward new life and was the first to open the door of heaven. He shall descend at the end of time to show our race where his royal palace is to be found.[1]

Baptism and the Eucharist are filled with eschatological meaning. They restore the condition of the first paradise and anticipate our future state. Through Baptism and the Eucharist humans are joined to the church and are in route to regain their country of origin. They become a pledge of salvation and a foretaste of happiness to come.[2] Ephrem in the <u>Commentary on the Diatesseron</u> explains:

> We have eaten Christ's body in place of the fruit of the Tree of Paradise, and his altar has taken the place of the Garden of Eden for us; the curse has been washed away by his innocent blood and in the hope of the resurrection we await the life that is to come, and indeed

133

we already walk in this new life, in that we already have a pledge of it.[3]

In the Maronite Sunday Office of Compline, the Church is addressed in the following prayer: "Blessed, holy and believing Church! ...Advance! Eat the Fire and the Bread. Drink also the Spirit in the Wine! For it is by the Fire and by the Spirit that you acquire beauty and that you enter with your Spouse into the wedding chamber." And in the Matins of Sunday, the Office chants: "Blessed are you who sleep, who have departed in the faith, for you have put on the sign of life, from the water; blessed are you, for the body and the blood that you have taken shall resurrect your members from the dust."[4]

The Maronite Office manifests a tension toward the heavenly kingdom and an "impatient desire" for the second coming. It awaits the heavenly community chanting an eternal liturgy to the 'Lamb of God'. In the meantime, human life has been transformed in the resurrection of Jesus which inaugurates the resurrection of the dead.

As indicated previously, there is a constant theme regarding the garments of light worn by Adam and Eve and lost at their sin. Baptism is seen as restoring this garment. The idea of a wedding garment for the future heavenly kingdom is also rooted in the Gospel. The Maronite Office reflects this eschatological theme. An example is found in the "sedro" of the Eveneing Office for the Sunday for the Faithful Departed: "...Also, Lord Christ, we ask that you grant to all those who rest in your hope, who have eaten your body and drunk your blood, to rise to meet you carrying their lighted lamps and dressed in wedding garments, that they be able to rest in the celestial dwellings of the Jerusalem on high..."

The eschatological thrust of the Eucharist is summarized in the Anaphora of St. Celestine which declares: "O Lord, grant that our sharing in this Holy Banquet may be a pledge of your unending Heavenly Feast, with your saints and chosen ones..."

### The Sleep of the Soul

The early Syriac fathers did offer a few descriptions of the condition of those who had died.[5] A convenient theory was to say that the dead went into a

134

sleep until final judgment. James of Serug in speaking
of the wise and foolish virgins claims that the good
virgins sleep with the oil of their good works with
them until the day of the Lord. The wicked sleep without oil and will stand and be ashamed on the last day.[6]

Another image taken from the Semetic tradition
is the idea that after death one must cross a river of
fire. The just are delivered while the evil are
burned. In making this crossing, James of Serug
teaches that help is received from the angels, the mysteries of Baptism and the Eucharist, and good works.
James petitions: "Let me pass through the sea of fire
in a boat of water. May baptism cover me from the
burning fire and spread its wings over the fire. May
the fountain of living water accompany me." Regarding
the Eucharist, James says: "When the odor of your body
and merciful blood, mixed in me, strikes the fire, may
it pull back from my members." Also, "If the gnashing
of teeth approaches me, may your body and blood, the
medicine of life, drive it away."[7]

The Maronite liturgy believes that the cross is
a bridge over the sea of fire. The "mazmoro" verse
preceeding the Scripture readings for the Liturgy for
the Departed chants: "May your cross be a bridge by
which the faithful departed, who wear the robe of Baptism, may be brought to the haven of eternal life."

'Coming to Harbor'

A symbol that is frequently used in Syriac
tradition to express the future kingdom is 'coming to
harbor'. However, in the East Syriac Church it could
also be applied to Christ as the 'harbor of peace'.
This latter meaning is connected with the Gospel story
of Peter sinking in the Sea of Galilee. In fact, in
the Syriac liturgical tradition the phrase coming to
harbor is often extended to Christ, the saints, and the
sacraments.

The Acts of Thomas view Christ as the haven for
those who accept baptism. Aphraat speaks of the world
as a ship directed by just men towards the harbor of
rest. Ephrem uses the image of harbor with an eschatological meaning, as well as the metaphor of pilot,
ship and sea. James of Serug sometimes uses the image
speaking of the end of life.[8]

## The future life

Regarding the condition of the next life, the School of Nisibis seems to have reasoned that in the next world we would contemplate the glorified humanity of Christ, in whom, as in a living image, we would see the invisible God.[9] Narsai claims that angels and humans will be united in love and will celebrate Christ as "the image of the hidden king". The hidden God is worshipped through the body of Christ, wherein they offer "the pure sacrifices of their minds." Narsai explains that God chose the body of Christ from the universe so that he might satisfy the need of the universe. Since it is impossible for creatures to reach the nature of God, God has "limited their inquiries to His visible image."[10]

Ephrem in his <u>Hymn on Paradise, No. 5</u> gives a description of the characteristics of the resurrected body:

A hundred times finer
and more subtil
is the body of the just
when they are risen, at the resurrection:
it resembles a thought
 that is able,
if it wills, to stretch out and expand,
or, should it wish, to contract and shrink:
or if it shrinks, it is somewhere,
if it expands, it is everywhere.[11]

### Conclusion

The Syriac Church had a deep faith in the completion of the work of salvation and the resurrection of all things by Christ in God. The key to the future of the Church and its individual members are the mysteries, especially Baptism and the Eucharist.

The focus of Syriac thought was on judgment day and therefore it was convenient to speak of the sleep of the dead until that day. On the other hand, there was also the tradition of a perilous journey to be made across the sea of fire with the possibility of falling into the fire because of one's sins.[12] Clothed by baptism, with the Eucharist as medicine of life, and the cross of Christ as a bridge, the just will come safely to harbor.

## Notes to Chapter Eleven

1. P. Gignoux, "Les doctrines eschatologiques de Narsai," L'Orient Syrien, vol. 11 (1966) pp. 325, 474, 487-8.

2. G. Saber, La Théologie Baptismale de Saint Ephrem, pp. 173-4.

3. S. Brock, "Mary and the Eucharist," Sobornost 1.2 (1979) p. 54.

4. J. Tabet, "L'Eschatologie dans l'Office Commun Maronite," Parole de l'Orient, vol. 2 (1971) pp. 6-25.

5. For a study of the condition of the soul after death, see the dissertation: F. Zayek, De Psychopannychia in Ecclesia Syriaca (unpublished doctoral dissertation at the Pontifical University of the Propagation of the Faith, Rome, 1948)

6. M. Guinan, "Where are the dead? in James of Serug," Orientalia Christiana Analecta, vol. 197, p. 542.

7. Ibid., pp. 543-5.

8. E.R. Hambye, "The Symbol of the 'Coming to the Harbour'," Orientalia Christiana Analecta, vol. 197, pp. 404-5.

9. W.F. Macomber, "The Theological Synthesis of Cyrus of Edessa," Orientalia Christiana Periodica, vol. 30, p. 383.

10. F. McLeod, "Man as the Image of God: its meaning and theological significance in Narsai," Theological Studies, vol. 42 (1981) pp. 462-3.

11. S. Brock, Harp of the Spirit, pp. 23-4.

12. Guinan, art. cit., pp. 548-9.

# CHAPTER TWELVE

## FAITH

With the redemptive work of Christ and the action of the Spirit culminating in Baptism, faith is engendered in our hearts. The Syriac writers view faith from several aspects.

Aphraat having established the teaching that Christ is the rock of faith declares in his Demonstration No. 1, on Faith that Christ the 'stone' is the foundation on which our faith is based. Aphraat continuing this image, speaks of a structure to be built by the person of faith:

> ...For first a man believes, and when he believes, he loves. When he loves, he hopes. When he hopes, he is justified. When he is justified, he is perfected. When he is perfected, he is consummated. And when his whole structure is raised up, consummated, and perfected, then he becomes a house and a temple for a dwelling-place of Christ...
> And when the house has become a dwelling-place, then the man begins to be anxious as to that which is required for Him who dwells in the building. [1]

We have already seen an aspect of Ephrem's teaching on faith when discussing divinization. In his Hymn on the Faith, No. 10, he declares: "By this truth <baptismal faith>, you are able to be united to celestial beings; further, you are united with God and formed in his image." Ephrem develops this idea of the renewal of God's image by teaching that "...faith is a second soul. As the body lives only by the soul, so the soul lives only by faith; if the soul entertains negation and doubt, it degrades itself into a corpse."[2]

According to R. Chesnut, Philoxenus develops this theme by teaching that the soul is that aspect of each person that participates in the life of the Spirit and should dwell in the region of heavenly beings. While the body knows through the senses, the soul by faith in the Holy Spirit can reach a knowledge of divine things. By faith, one can see the reality lying under the visible world, can perceive the new man who comes into existence through Baptism, and understands that the bread and wine of the Eucharist are the body and blood of God.[3]

Ephrem, as we have already indicated, links faith through baptism with each member of the Trinity. He also assures the believer that the Trinity will serve as a protection and support when faith is tested. In his Hymn on the Faith, No. 13, he teaches:

I presented my faith to the Father and he imprinted it with his Fatherhood;
I presented it to the Son and he mingled it with his being
and the Holy Spirit, too, sanctified it
and fashioned in it the mystery which sanctifies everything.

Faith which is not thus imprinted <"rushma"> goes astray.
Let us prepare ourselves for affliction should it come:
though our spirit suffer, our soul be separated, our body burnt,
what can overcome us?

On Three Names hangs our Baptism;
by three mysteries has our faith been victorious;
three names has our Lord consigned to his Twelve,
Names in which we have taken refuge![4]

In a beautiful image, Ephrem describes the gift of faith as ultimately the fruit of the cross, the tree of life. In his Hymn on the Pearl, No. 4, Ephrem explains:

The thief sought to possess the faith, but the faith possessed him; and enthroned him in Paradise. He lives on the cross, this tree of life, of which faith is the fruit, and in place of Adam, it is he who eats of it.[5]

For the Syriac Fathers, faith is essentially a divine gift granted through the redemption of Christ. While human freedom of choice is implied, there is no existential analysis of how the act of faith occurs. As part of the process of divinization, the possession of faith by humans is intended from the time of creation. In this view, the truth of faith is the goal of

140

the human mind, although it is beyond human capacity.

## Conclusion

Therefore, we can conclude this study, as we began, by reflecting on the paradox of the knowledge of faith and the hiddeness of God. While the realm of the Holy is distinct unto itself and radically inaccessible to human reason, God's Word makes the Father knowable, and creation being made through the Word is in its very nature the self-revelation of God. The Incarnation is both the fulfillment of revelation, and the renewal of the process of divinization. The Church and the Mysteries continue Christ's redemptive work, and in the sanctifying event itself divine realities are being disclosed. Thus baptismal faith is the climax of what it is to be human in the presence of God, and grants angelic knowledge of that Reality that must always remain Mystery.

## Notes to Chapter Twelve

1. Nicene and Post-Nicene Fathers, p. 346.

2. G. Saber, La Théologie Baptismale de Saint Ephrem, pp. 56-7.

3. R. Chesnut, Three Monophysite Christologies, pp. 71-2.

4. Cited by P. Yousif, "St. Ephrem on Symbols in Nature: Faith, the Trinity and the Cross (Hymn on the Faith, No. 18)," Eastern Churches Review, vol. 10 (1978) p. 56.

5. F. Graffin, "Les Hymnes sur le perle de Saint Ephrem," L'Orient Syrien, vol. 12 (1967) pp. 133 ff.

BIBLIOGRAPHY

Albert, M., "Mimro de Jacques de Saroug sur la Synagogue et l'église," L'Orient Syrien, vol. 7
(1962) pp. 143-62.

Anaphora Book of the Syriac-Maronite Church of Antioch. Youngstown: Liturgical Commission of
the Diocese of St. Maron, 1978.

Beck, E., "Le Baptême chez saint Ephrem," L'Orient
Syrien vol. 1 (1956) pp. 111-36.

Beck, E., "Symbolum-Mysteriem bei Aphrahat und Ephrem," Oriens Christianus, vol. 42 (1958) pp.
19-40.

Beggiani, S., "Christian Initiation in the Eastern
Churches," Living Light, vol. 11 (1974) pp.
536--47.

Botte, B, "Le baptême dans l'Église Syrienne," L'O-
rient Syrien, vol. 1 (1956) pp. 137-55.

Botte, B., "La Formule d'Ordination 'La Grace Divine'
dans les rites orientaux," L'Orient Syrien,
vol. 2 (1957) pp. 285-96.

Botte, B., "Postbaptismal Anointing in the Ancient
Patriarchate of Antioch," Studies on Syrian
Baptismal Rites, ed. by Jacob Vellian. Kot-
tayam: C.M.S. Press, 1973.

Breydy, M., "Precisions liturgiques syro-maronites sur
le sacerdoce," Oriens Christianus, vol. 48
(1964) pp. 57-76.

Brock, S., "Baptismal themes in the writings of Jacob
of Serugh," Orientalia Christiana Analecta,
vol. 205 (1978) pp. 325-47.

Brock, S., "Consignation in the West Syrian Baptismal
Rite," Studies on Syrian Baptismal Rites, pp.
100-118.

Brock, S., "Ephrem's letter to Publius," Le Museon,
vol. 89 (1976) pp. 216-305.

143

Brock, S., "The Epiklesis in the Antiochene Baptismal Ordines," <u>Orientalia Christiana Analecta</u>, vol. 197, pp. 183-215.

Brock, S., "Greek into Syriac and Syriac into Greek," <u>Journal of the Syriac Academy</u>, vol. 3 (1977) pp. 1-17 <or Arabic numbers 422-406>.

Brock, S. <u>The Harp of the Spirit</u>. Fellowiship of St. Alban and St. Sergius, 1975.

Brock, S., "Jacob of Edessa's Discourse on the Myron," <u>Oriens Christianus</u>, vol. 63 (1979) pp. 20-36.

Brock, S., "Jacob of Serugh on the Veil of Moses," <u>Sobornost</u>, vol. 3 (1981) pp. 70-85.

Brock, S., "Marie dans la tradition Syriaque," <u>Lettre de Ligugé</u>, vol. 189 (1978) pp. 5-15.

Brock, S., "Mary and the Eucharist," <u>Sobornost</u>, vol. 1 (1979) pp. 50-59.

Brock, S., "The Mysteries Hidden in the Side of Christ," <u>Sobornost</u>, 7.6 (1978) pp. 462-72.

Brock, S., "A New Syrian Baptismal Ordo Attributed to Timothy of Alexandria," <u>Studies on Syrian Baptismal Rites</u>, pp. 72-84.

Brock, S., "The Poet as Theologian," <u>Sobornost</u> 7.4 (1977) pp. 243-250.

Brock, S., "The Poetic Artistry of St. Ephrem: an Analysis of H. Azym. III," <u>Parole de l'Orient</u>, vols. 6-7 (1975-6) pp. 21-8.

Brock, S., "St. Ephrem on Christ as Light in Mary and in the Jordan: Hymni De Ecclesia 36," <u>Eastern Churches Review</u>, vol. 7 (1975) pp. 137-44.

Brock, S., "A Short Melkite Baptismal Service in Syriac," <u>Parole de l'Orient</u>, vol. 3 (1972) pp. 119-130.

Brock, S., "The Syriac baptismal ordines, with special reference to the anointings," <u>Studia Liturgica</u>, vol. 13 (1978) pp. 177-83.

Brock, S., "The Syrian Baptismal Rites," Concilium,
    vol. 22 (1979) pp. 98-104.

Brock, S., "The Transition to a Post-Baptismal Anoin-
    ting in the Antiochene Rite," The Sacrifice of
    Praise, ed. by Bryan D. Spinks. Rome: Edizioni
    Liturgiche, 1981, pp. 215-25.

Brock, S., "World and Sacrament in the Writings of the
    Syrian Fathers," Sobornost, 6.10 (1974) pp.
    685-96.

Burkitt, F.C. Early Eastern Christianity. London,
    1904.

Camelot, P.-T., "Lumière, Étude Patristique, II,"
    Dictionnaire de Spiritualite, vol. 9, cols.
    1150-8.

Chesnut, R. Three Monophysite Christologies: Se-
    verus of Antioch, Philoxenus of Mabbug, and
    Jacob of Sarug. London: Oxford University
    Press, 1976.

Connolly, R.H. The Liturgical Homililes of Narsai.
    Cambridge: Cambridge University Press, 1970.

Cyril of Jerusalem's Lectures on the Christian Sac-
    raments. transl. by F.L. Cross. London:
    S.P.C.K., 1951.

Dalmais, I.H., "L'Héritage Antiochien de l'Église
    Maronite," Melto, vol. 3 (1967) pp. 61-70.

Dalmais, I.H., "Source Baptismale et Mystère Pascal
    d'après les homélies de Severe d'Antioche sur
    'la preparation quadragesimale de l'entree au
    baptistere'," Parole de l'Orient, vols. 6-7
    (1975-6) pp. 349-56.

de Halleux, A., "Mar Ephrem Theologien," Parole de
    l'Orient vol. 4 (1973) pp. 35-54.

de Vries, W., "La Conception de l'Église chez les Sy-
    riens séparés de Rome (Les Syriens du patriarcat
    d'Antioche)," L'Orient Syrien, vol. 2 (1957)
    pp. 111-24.

de Vries, W., "La Conception de l'Église chez les Sy-
    riens séparés  de Rome (Les Syriens du catholi-

cosat de Seleucie-Ctesiphon)," L'Orient Syrien, vol. 3 (1958) 149-64.

de Vries, W., "Théologie des Sacraments chez les Syriens monophysites," L'Orient Syrien, vol. 8
(1963) pp. 261-88.

Desreumaux, Alain, "Une Homélie Syriaque Anonyme sur
la Nativité," Parole de l'Orient, vols. 6-7
(1975-6) pp. 195-212.

Duncan, E. Baptism in the Demonstrations of Aphraates the Persian Sage. Washington: Catholic
University Press, 1945.

El-Khoury, Nabil, "Gen. 1, 26 -- Dans l'Interpretation
de Saint Ephrem, ou la Relations de l'Homme à
Dieu," Orientalia Christiana Analecta, vol.
205 (1978) pp. 199-205.

Fenqitho: A Treasury of Feasts According to the Syriac-Maronite Church of Antioch. Diocese of
St. Maron -- U.S.A., 1980.

Finn, T. The Liturgy of Baptism in the Baptismal
Instructions of St. John Chrysostom. Washington: Catholic University Press, 1967.

Fox, Douglas J. The "Matthew-Luke Commentary" of
Philoxenus. Missoula: Scholars' Press, 1979.

Gavin, F., "The Sleep of the Soul in the early Syriac
Church," Journal of the American Oriental Society, vol. 40 (1920) pp. 103-20.

Gelineau, J., "Données Liturgiques Contenues dans les
sept madrosé 'de la nuit' de Saint Ephrem,"
L'Orient Syrien vol. 5 (1960) pp. 107-21.

Gemayel, P. Prière du Croyant selon l'année litur-
gique Maronite. 3 vols. Beyrouth, 1968.

Gignoux, P., "Les doctrines eschatologiques de Narsai," L'Orient Syrien, vol. 11 (1966) pp.
321-53; 461-88; vol. 12 (1967) pp. 23-54.

Gignoux, P., "Homélie de Narsai sur la creation d'Adam
et d'Ève et sur la transgression de commande-
ment," L'Orient Syrien, vol. 7 (1962) pp. 307-
36.

Gignoux, P., "Homélie de Narsai sur la Création du Monde," L'Orient Syrien, vol. 7 (1962) pp. 477-506.

Gignoux, P., "Homélie de Narsai sur le mot "Au Commencement" et sur l'essence Divine," L'Orient Syrien, vol. 8 (1963) pp. 227-50.

Gogan, Brian, "Penance Rites of the West Syrian Liturgy: Some Liturgical and Theological Implications," The Irish Theological Quarterly, vol. 42 (1975) p. 182-96.

Graffin, F., "Explication des sens mystiques des membres du corps du Christ," Parole de l'Orient (1970) pp. 255-80.

Graffin, F., "Hymnes inédites de saint Ephrem sur la Virginité," L'Orient Syrien, vol. 6 (1961) pp. 213-42.

Graffin, F., "La Catéchèse de Sévère d'Antioche," L'Orient Syrien, vol. 5 (1960) pp. 47-54.

Graffin, F., "Les Hymnes de Saint Ephrem sur la perle," L'Orient Syrien, vol. 12 (1967) pp. 129-49.

Graffin, F., "Le thème de la perle chez Jacques de Saroug," L'Orient Syrien, vol. 12 (1967) pp. 355-70.

Graffin, F. "L'Eucharistie chez Saint Ephrem," Parole de l'Orient, vol. 4 (1973) pp. 93-121.

Graffin, F., "Recherches sur le thème de l'église-épouse: dans les liturgies et la litterature patristique de langue syriaque," L'Orient Syrien, vol. 3 (1958) pp. 317-36.

Gribomont, J., "Les Hymnes de Saint Ephrem sur la Paques," Melto, vol. 3 (1967) pp. 147-82.

Gribomont, J., "Le triomphe de Pacques d'après S. Ephrem," Parole de l'Orient, vol. 4 (1973) 147-89.

Guinan, M. The Eschatology of James of Sarug. (Dissertation, Catholic University of America, 1971)

Guinan, M., "Where are the dead? in James pf Serug," *Orientalia Christiana Analecta*, vol. 197, pp. 541-50.

Hambye, E.R., "The Symbol of the 'Coming to Harbour'," *Orientalia Christiana Analecta*, vol. 197, pp. 401-11.

Harb, P., "La Conception pneumatologique chez Philoxene de Mabboug," *Melto*, vol. 5 (1969) pp. 5-15.

Harb, P., "Le role exerce par Philoxene de Mabboug sur l'évolution de la morale dans l'église syrienne," *Parole de l'Orient*, vol. 1 (1970) pp. 27-48.

Hastings, A., "The Sacramentality of the Church," *Eastern Churches Quarterly*, vol. 16 (1964) pp. 219-25.

Jansma, T., "Aphraates' Demonstration VII #18 and 20: Some Observations on the Discourse on Penance," *Parole de l'Orient*, vol. 5 (1974) pp. 21-48.

Jansma, T., "Ephraem on Exodus II, 5: Reflections on the Interplay of Freewill and Divine Providence," *Orientalia Christiana Periodica*, vol. 39 (1973) pp. 5-28.

Jansma, T., "Encore le credo de Jacques de Saroug: Nouvelles recherches sur l'argument historique concernant son orthodoxie," *L'Orient Syrien*, vol. 10 (1965) p. 75-88; 193-236; 331-70; 475-510.

Jansma, T., "Études sur la Pensée de Narsai," *L'Orient Syrien*, vol. 11 (1966) pp. 147-68; 265-90; 393-430.

Jansma, T., "Narsai and Ephraem: Some observations on Narsai's Homilies on Creation and Ephraem's Hymns on Faith," *Parole de l'Orient*, vol. 1 (1970) pp. 49-68.

Jansma, T., "Une homélie anonyme sur l'effusion du Esprit," *L'Orient Syrien*, vol. 6 (1961) pp. 157-78.

John Chrysostom. *Baptismal Instructions*. transl.

by P. Harkins. London: Longmans's Green and Co., 1963.

Khalifé-hachem, E., "Homélie Metrique de Jacques de Saroug sur l'amour," Parole de l'Orient, vol. 1 (1970) pp. 281-99.

Khalifé-hachem, E., "Office Maronite du Grand Dimanche de la Résurrection: Texte du Ramso et Commentaire," Parole de l'Orient, vols. 6-7 (1975-6) pp. 281-308.

Khouri-Sarkis, G., "Introduction aux Églises de langue syriaque," L'Orient Syrien, vol. 1 (1956) pp. 3-35.

Khouri-Sarkis, G., "Le sommeil des ames," L'Orient Syrien, vol. 3 (1958) p. 489-94.

Khouri-Sarkis, G., "Prieres et ceremonies du bapteme, selon le rituel de l'Eglise Syrienne d'Antioche," L'Orient Syrien, vol. 1 (1956) pp. 156-84.

Klijn, A.F.J., "Baptism in the Acts of Thomas," Studies on Syrian Baptismal Rites, pp.57-62.

Kronholm, T. Motifs from Genesis 1-11 in the Genuine Hymns of Ephrem the Syrian. Uppsala: Almqvist & Wiksell, 1978.

Kruger, P., "Le sommeil des âmes dans l'oeuvre de Narsai," L'Orient Syrien, vol. 4 (1959) pp. 193-210.

Lavenant, R., "Trois Hymnes de saint Ephrem sur le paradis," L'Orient Syrien, vol. 5 (1960) pp. 33-46.

Lectionary, Syriac-Maronite Church (The Seasons). Detroit: Diocese of St. Maron -- U.S.A., 1976.

Lecuyer, J., "La Théologie de l'anaphore selon les peres de l'école d'Antioche," L'Orient Syrien, vol. 6 (1961) pp. 385-412.

Leloir, L. Doctrines et Methodes de S. Ephrem d'après son Commentaire de l'Evangile Concordant. Corpus Scriptorum Christianorm Orientalium. vol. 220 (Subsidia 18). Louvain, 1961.

Leloir, L., "Symbolisme et parallelisme chez Ephrem,"
À la rencontre de Dieu, memorial Albert Gelin,
(Lyon: Editions Xavier Mappus, 1961) pp. 363-74.

Le Roy, J. Les manuscripts syriaques a peintures,
conserves dans les bibliotheques d'Europe et
d'Orient, 2 vols. Paris, 1964.

Ligier, L., "Dimension Personnelle et Dimension Communitaire de la Pénitence en Orient," La Maison
Dieu, vol. 90, pp. 155-87.

Ligier, L., "Le Sacrement de Pénitence selon la Tradition Orientale," Nouvelle Revue Theolo-
gique, vol. 89 (1967) pp. 940-77.

Ligier, L. "Penitence et Eucharistie en Orient,"
Orientalia Christiana Periodica, vol. 29, pp.
5-77.

Macomber, W.F., "An Anaphora Prayer Composed by
Theodore of Mopsuestia," Parole de l'Orient,
vols. 6-7 (1975-6) pp. 341-8.

Macomber, W.F., "A History of the Chaldean Mass,"
Worship, vol. 51 (1977) pp. 107-20.

Macomber, W.F., "The Theological Synthesis of Cyrus of
Edessa, an East Syrian Theologian of the Mid-
Sixth Century," Orientalia Christiana Perio-
dica, vol. 30 (1964) pp. 5-38; 363-84.

Macomber, W.F., "A Theory on the Origins of the Syrian, Maronite, and Chaldean Rites," Orientalia
Christiana Periodica, vol. 39 (1973) pp. 235-
42.

Mateos, J., "Prières syriennes d'absolution du VII-IX
siècles," Orientalia Christiana Periodica,
vol. 34 (1968) pp. 252-80.

McLeod, F., "Man as the Image of God: its meaning and
theological significance in Narsai," Theological Studies, vol. 42 (1981) pp. 458-67.

Mingana, A., ed. Commentary of Theodore of Mopsuestia on the Sacraments of Baptism and the
Eucharist. Woodbrooke Studies, No. 6. Cambridge, 1933.

Mingana, A., ed. Early Christian Mystics. Woodbrooke Studies, No. 7. Cambridge: W. Heffer &
Sons, Ltd., 1934.

Mitchell, L., "Four Fathers on Baptism: St. John Chrysostom, St. Ephraem, Theodore of Mopsuestia,
Narsai," Studies on Syrian Baptismal Rites,
pp. 37-56.

Mouhanna, A., "Consecration de l'eau dans la liturgie
Baptismale Maronite," Parole de l'Orient, vol.
8 (1977-8) pp. 217-33.

Mouhanna, A., "Le Rite du Pardon dans l'Église Maronite," Parole de l'Orient, vols. 6-7 (1975-
6) pp. 309-24.

Mouhanna, A. Les Rites de l'Initiation dans l'Eglise Maronite. Rome: Pontificium Institutum
Orientalium Studiorum, 1978.

Murray, R., "A Hymn of St. Ephrem to Christ," Sobornost, 11.1 (1979) pp. 39-50.

Murray, R., "A Hymn of St. Ephrem to Christ on the
Incarnation, the Holy Spirit, and the Sacraments," Eastern Churches Review, vol. 3
(1970-1) pp. 142-50.

Murray, R., "Mary, the Second Eve in the Early Syriac
Fathers," Eastern Churches Review, vol. 3
(1970-1) pp. 372-84.

Murray, R., "Recent Studies in Early Symbolic Theology," Heythrop Journal, vol. 6 (1965) pp.
412-33.

Murray, R., "The Rock and the House on the Rock,"
Orientalia Christiana Periodica, vol. 30, pp.
315-62.

Murray, R., "St. Ephrem the Syrian on Church Unity,"
Eastern Churches Quarterly, vol. 15 (1963) pp.
164-76.

Murray, R. Symbols of Church and Kingdom. London:
Cambridge University Press, 1975.

Murray, R. "The Theory of Symbolism in St. Ephrem's

Theology," <u>Parole de l'Orient</u>, vols. 6-7 (1975-6) pp. 1-20.

Noujaim, Guy, "Essai sur quelques aspects de la philo-sophie d'Ephrem de Nisibe," <u>Parole de l'O-rient</u>, vol. 9 (1979-80) pp. 27-50.

Ortiz de Urbina, I., "Le Paradis eschatologiques d'ap-rès Saint Ephrem," <u>Orientalia Christiana Perio-dica</u>, vol. 21 (1955) pp. 467-72.

Outtier, D., "Contribution a l'Étude de la Prehistoire des collections d'hymns d'Ephrem," <u>Parole de l'Orient</u>, vols. 6-7 (1975-6) pp. 49-61.

Raes, A., "Le consentement matrimonial dans les rites orientaux," <u>Ephemeriedes Liturgicae</u> vol. 47 (1933) pp. 34-47, 126-40, 249-59, 431-45; vol. 48 (1934) pp. 80-94, 310-18.

Raes, A. <u>Le Mariage, sa célébration et sa spiritu-alité dans les Églises d'Orient</u>. Editions de Chevetogne, 1958.

Raes, A., "Où se trouve la Confirmation dans le rite syro-oriental?" <u>L'Orient Syrien</u>, vol. 1 (1956) pp. 239-54.

Raes, A., "Une rite pénitentiel avant la communion dans les liturgies syriennes," <u>L'Orient Sy-rien</u>, vol. 10 (1965) pp. 107-22.

Ratcliff, E.C., "The Old Syrian Baptismal Tradition and its Resettlement Under the Influence of Jerusalem in the Fourth Century," <u>Studies on Syrian Baptismal Rites</u>, pp. 85-99.

Reine, F. <u>The Eucharistic Doctrine and Liturgy of the Mystagogical Catecheses of Theodore of Mop-suestia</u>. Washington: Catholic University Press, 1942.

Saber, G. <u>La Théologie Baptismale de Saint Ephrem</u>. Kaslik, 1974.

Saber, G., "La Typologie Sacramentaire et Baptismale de Saint Ephrem," <u>Parole de l'Orient</u>, vol. 4 (1973) pp. 73-91.

Sauget, J.-M., "Le Mariage dans le rite syrien occi-

dental," <u>L'Orient Syrien</u>, vol. 2 (1957) pp.
3-14.

Sauget, J.-M., "Prières et cérémonies du mariage syrien occidental," <u>L'Orient Syrien</u>, vol. 2
(1957) pp. 15-37.

Sauget, J.-M., "Une Homélie Syriaque sur la pécheresse
attribuée a un évêque Jean," <u>Parole de l'O
rient</u>, vols. 6-7 (1975-6) p. 159-94.

Sed, N., "Les Hymnes sur le paradis de saint Ephrem
juives," <u>Le Museon</u>, vol. 81 (1968) pp. 455-
501.

<u>A Select Library of Nicene and Post-Nicene Fathers of
The Christian Church</u>. (Second Series) ed. by
P. Schaff and H. Wace. Grand Rapids: Wm. B.
Eerdmans Publishing Company, 1964.

Slim, J., "Hymne I de Saint Ephrem sur la Résurrection," <u>L'Orient Syrien</u>, vol. 12 (1967) pp.
505-14.

Tabet, J., "L'eschatologie dans l'Office Commun Maronite," <u>Parole de l'Orient</u>, vol. 2 (1971) pp.
5-29.

Tabet, J. <u>L'Office Commun Maronite: Étude du Lilyo</u>
<u>et du Safro</u>. Kaslik, 1972.

Taft, R., "The Continuity of Tradition in a World of
Liturgical Change: The Eastern Liturgical Experience," <u>Seminarium</u>, vol. 27 (1975) pp.
445-59.

Tanghe, A., "L'Eucharistie pour la rémission des
Péches," <u>Irenikon</u>, vol. 34 (1961) pp. 165-81.

Tanghe, A., "Memra de Philoxene de Mabboug sur l'in-
habitation du Saint Esprit," <u>Le Museon</u>, vol. 83
(1970) pp. 209-36.

Teixidor, J., "Le thème de la descente aux enfers chez
saint Ephrem," <u>L'Orient Syrien</u>, vol. 6 (1961)
pp. 25-40.

Terzoli, R., "Âme et Esprit chez Aphraate," <u>Parole
de l'Orient</u>, vol. 3 (1972) pp. 105-18.

Tonneau, R.M., "Le rite primitif du Baptême," L'O rient Syrien, vol. 1 (1956) pp. 333-44.

Van Overstraeten, J.G., "Le Rite de l'Onction des Époux dans la liturgie Copte du Mariage," Parole de l'Orient, vol. 5 (1974) pp. 49-93.

Van Overstraeten, J.G., "Les Liturgies Nuptiales des Églises de Langue Syriaque et le Mystère de l'Église-Épouse," Parole de l'Orient, vol. 8 (1977-8) pp. 235-310.

Van Vossel, V., "Le terme et la notion de 'sceau' dans le rituel baptismal des syriens orientaux," L'Orient Syrien, vol. 10 (1965) pp. 237-60.

Verghese, P., "The Relation between Baptism,'Confirmation' and the Eucharist in the Syrian Orthodox Church," Studia Liturgica, vol. 4 (1965) pp. 81-93.

Voobus, A., "The Institution of the Benai Qeiama and Benat Qeiama in the Ancient Syrian Church," Church History, vol. 30, (1961) pp. 19-27.

Wainwright, G., "The Baptismal Eucharist before Nicaea," Studia Liturgica, vol. 4 (1965) pp. 9-36.

Wainwright, G. Christian Initiation. Richmond: John Knox Press, 1969.

Winkler, G., "The Original Meaning of the Prebaptismal Anointing and Its Implications," Worship, vol. 52 (1978) pp. 24-45.

Yousif, P., "La Croix de Jesus et le Paradis d'Eden dans la typologie biblique de saint Ephrem," Parole de l'Orient, vols. 6-7 (1975-6) pp. 29-48.

Yousif, P., "Le Symbolisme de la croix dans la nature chez Saint Ephrem," Orientalia Christiana Analecta, vol. 205, pp. 207-27.

Yousif, P., "St. Ephrem on Symbols in Nature: Faith, the Trinity and the Cross (Hymns on Faith, No. 18)", Eastern Churches Review, vol. 10 (1978) pp. 52-60.

Yousif, P., "Symbolisme Christologique dans la Bible et dans la Nature chez S. Ephrem de Nisibe," _Parole de l'Orient_, vol. 8 (1977-8) pp. 5-66.

Zayek, F. _De Psychopannychia in Ecclesia Syriaca._ (doctoral dissertation, Pii Instituti S. Joannis Damasceni) Rome, 1948.

Ziade, I., "Syrienne (Église). Theologie Sacramentaire," _Dictionnaire de Théologie Catholique_, vol. 14, 2, cols. 3047-70.